HOLT

Elements of Language

THIRD COURSE

Think as a Writer: Interactive Grammar WorkText

Grammar Practice for Chapters 1–20

- Choices Activities
- Literary Models
- Writing Applications
- Grammar Worksheets and Lessons

HOLT, RINEHART AND WINSTON

Printed in the United States of America

ISBN 978-0-03-099562-0
ISBN 0-03-099562-0

13 14 15 0607 26 25 24 23 22 21 20 19

4500779673

Table of Contents

Table of Contents *(continued)*

Table of Contents *(continued)*

Section 2: Practice with Sentences and Paragraphs

Table of Contents *(continued)*

Table of Contents *(continued)*

About This Book

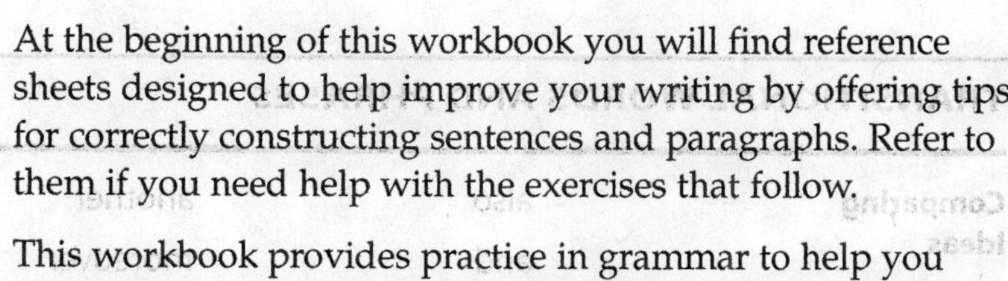

At the beginning of this workbook you will find reference sheets designed to help improve your writing by offering tips for correctly constructing sentences and paragraphs. Refer to them if you need help with the exercises that follow.

This workbook provides practice in grammar to help you improve your writing skills. **Section 1: Applying Grammar, Usage, and Mechanics** provides you with activities and writing applications to help you improve the grammar in your written work. The practice worksheets in **Section 2: Practice with Sentences and Paragraphs** and **Section 3: More Practice with Combining Sentences** will help you write grammatically correct sentences and provide you with help in combining sentences to make your writing more interesting.

Section 1: Applying Grammar, Usage, and Mechanics has the following features:

- **Choices Activities** These activities give you an opportunity to explore a topic in grammar in a way that interests you most. Art, mathematics, creative writing, and more are used to help you learn grammar concepts.
- **Literary Models** You will use a literature selection to examine why authors use the techniques they do, and you will write your own examples of authors' styles. These worksheets illustrate the difference between creative writing and formal writing.
- **Writing and Proofreading Applications** These worksheets provide you with a writing activity and give tips on how to complete the activity using the steps in the writing process, from prewriting to proofreading. The section also provides you with ways to extend your writing assignment. The proofreading applications give guidelines and practice to help you improve your writing.

Section 2: Practice with Sentences and Paragraphs and **Section 3: More Practice with Combining Sentences** contain worksheets to help you practice writing grammatical and effective sentences. Practice worksheets help you improve your writing by providing you with practice in the following:

- revising and proofreading
- combining sentences
- identifying fragments and run-ons
- identifying stringy and wordy sentences.

Varying types of sentences and correcting troublesome sentences will make your writing more interesting.

Transitional Words and Phrases

TRANSITIONAL WORDS AND PHRASES			
Comparing Ideas	also and	another moreover	similarly too
Contrasting Ideas	still but yet	in spite of instead however	on the other hand although nevertheless
Showing Cause and Effect	for since so	so that because thus	as a result therefore consequently
Showing Chronological Order	after then next before	eventually finally first meanwhile	at once at last thereafter when
Showing Spatial Order	into next over in here	above across behind before inside	beyond down around there under
Showing Order of Importance	first last	mainly then	to begin with more important

Varying Sentence Beginnings

SINGLE-WORD MODIFIERS

Excitedly, Marcia opened her presents.

[adverb]

Hungry, the family stopped at the restaurant.

[adjective]

PHRASES

With tears of joy, Carla received her prize.

[prepositional phrase]

Smiling happily, Tanya told us the good news.

[participial phrase]

To make good grades, you must study.

[infinitive phrase]

SUBORDINATE CLAUSES

Because the coach insisted, the team ran ten laps.

[adverb clause]

When Tom found the kitten on his doorstep, he decided to keep it.

[adverb clause]

Conjunctive Adverbs / Subordinating Conjunctions

COMMON CONJUNCTIVE ADVERBS		
accordingly	however	next
also	incidentally	nonetheless
anyhow	indeed	otherwise
anyway	instead	still
beside	likewise	then
consequently	meanwhile	therefore
finally	moreover	thus
furthermore	nevertheless	

COMMON SUBORDINATING CONJUNCTIONS		
after	before	unless
although	how	until
as	if	when
as if	in order that	whenever
as long as	since	where
as soon as	so that	wherever
as though	than	whether
because	though	while

Symbols for Revising and Proofreading

Symbol	Example	Meaning of Symbol
≡	Fifty-first street (≡ under s)	Capitalize a lowercase letter.
/	Jerry's /Aunt	Lowercase a capital letter.
∧	differ^e^ant	Change a letter.
∧	the capital ^of^ Ohio	Insert a missing word, letter, or punctuation mark.
∧‾	beside the ^lake^ ~~river~~	Replace a word.
ℊ	Where's the ~~the~~ key?	Leave out a word, letter, or punctuation mark.
ℊ͡	an invisib~~l~~le guest	Leave out and close up.
⁀‿	a close friend ship	Close up space.
∽	thier	Change the order of letters.
(tr)	Avoid having too many corrections (of your paper) in the final version ^	Transfer the circled words. (Write *tr* in nearby margin.)
¶	¶"Hi," he smiled.	Begin a new paragraph.
⊙	Stay well⊙	Add a period.
∧,	Of course ^, you may be wrong.	Add a comma.
#	ice^#^hockey	Add a space.
(:)	one of the following(:)	Add a colon.
∧;	Maria Simmons, M.D.^; Jim Fiorello, Ph.D.	Add a semicolon.
=	a great=grandmother	Add a hyphen.
∨'	Paul^'^s car	Add an apostrophe.
(stet)	On the fifteenth of ~~July~~	Keep the crossed-out material. (Write *stet* in nearby margin.)

Section 1: Applying Grammar, Usage, and Mechanics

NAME CLASS DATE

Choices: Exploring Parts of Speech

The following activities challenge you to find a connection between the parts of speech and the world around you. Do the activity below that suits your personality best, and then share your discoveries with your class.

TIME LINE

A First Time for Everything

What is the history of each part of speech? Make a time line showing when the terms *noun, pronoun, adjective, verb, adverb, preposition, conjunction,* and *interjection* were first used in English. (HINT: Look in the *Oxford English Dictionary.*) Then, with your teacher's approval, post your time line in the classroom.

RESEARCH

Deep Roots

Look up the etymologies of the parts of speech—*noun, pronoun, adjective, verb, adverb, preposition, conjunction,* and *interjection.* Name the root words of each term, and give your classmates a brief explanation of each.

VISUAL PRESENTATION

The Ins and Outs

Create a Venn diagram showing the relationships between transitive and intransitive verbs and action and linking verbs. Include example sentences for each section of the diagram. Explain the diagram so that everyone understands. Write several additional examples of verbs in sentences on the chalkboard, and help your classmates place them correctly in your diagram.

CREATIVE WRITING

Metamorphosing Metaphors

Write a poem composed mostly of words that can function as different parts of speech. Use each of these words as at least two parts of speech or even more, if you can!

ETYMOLOGY

Star Quality

Is grammar glamorous? Don't answer yet. First, look up the definition of the word *glamour,* and then decide. Next, write a short report detailing your findings and give copies to your classmates.

DRAMA

Shorthand

Compose a dialogue between two or more people. Here's the catch: Use only two parts of speech—any two you like. Tell your classmates to sit back and enjoy the show.

CREATIVE WRITING

A Household Word

Wouldn't it be great to have a word based on you or your name enter the English language? If there were a word based on your name, what would it be? What would its part of speech be? Write a story about how this word came into being.

CONTEST

Chameleon Conjunctions

Have a contest: Who can find a word that can function as the most parts of speech? The winner must present complete sentences appropriately using his or her word as each part of speech.

WORLD LANGUAGES

When in Rome

In today's world, many people speak more than one language. Ask around and find a few multilingual speakers. Ask them, "Do other languages use different parts of speech than English uses? If so, what are they?" Report your findings to the class.

ORIGINAL PROJECTS

None of the Above

If none of the projects above grab you, make up your own. Convert the parts of speech into colors, and color-code a paragraph. Translate the parts of speech into musical notes, code a paragraph, and play it. Identify some nouns, verbs, and adjectives that science has created in the last fifty years. Invent a new part of speech. Write a personality profile of a verb. Whatever you decide to do, get your teacher's approval first.

Literary Model: Using Nouns to Create Setting

Pressing herself flat against the rear wall of Señor Aguilar's hotel near the Avenida Ruiz, Lupita Torres bided her time. When she heard the doors of the big green *yanqui* car shut and the tourist start the engine, she slid forward, scraping her back on the rough white stucco.

—from *Lupita Mañana* by Patricia Beatty

EXERCISE A

1. On the lines below, write each noun that appears in the above paragraph. Then, circle the proper nouns. (Note: One noun is in the possessive case; it ends with an apostrophe and an *s*.)

2. The nouns work together to create the sense of a particular cultural setting. What specific information do they give about the setting?

EXERCISE B Rewrite the paragraph, replacing most of the nouns with nouns of your own choosing. Use nouns that create a different cultural setting. You may also change an adjective or two.

Literary Model (continued)

EXERCISE C Write a paragraph describing two people walking up to the front door of your dream house. Use common and proper nouns to communicate a clear setting. For example, the house may be on a busy street in Paris, France, or it may be nestled among the sand dunes of a remote beach in North Carolina. Underline each noun.

EXERCISE D If you replaced all the proper nouns in your paragraph with common nouns, would the paragraph create the same specific setting and tone? Explain why or why not.

Writing Application: Description

A word of advice that all writers learn is "Show—don't tell." Using well-chosen adjectives and adverbs, writers bring their subjects into sharp focus, giving concrete edges to their ideas and adding interest to their writing, just as a painter uses detail to create a lifelike portrait.

LESS INTERESTING The batter ran the bases after hitting the home run.

MORE INTERESTING The sweat-soaked batter triumphantly ran the bases after hitting the home run.

Think of other adjectives and adverbs that you could use to help readers "see" the action described in the sentence above.

Writing Activity

You've probably heard of Leonardo da Vinci's famous *Mona Lisa,* which he finished painting in 1506. Find a picture of this painting, and write a paragraph describing the painting. Mona Lisa's smile has been called mysterious and playful—how will you describe it? Finish your description with your thoughts on what Leonardo's subject might have been thinking as she smiled. Include in your writing at least three carefully chosen adjectives and at least three interesting adverbs.

PREWRITING Observe the painting carefully, jotting down whatever descriptive words come to mind as you look at it. You might even hold an imaginary conversation with Mona Lisa, asking her what she is thinking and writing what she might reply.

WRITING Decide how you will arrange your descriptive details. Will you describe the whole painting and then focus on details, or start in the center of the painting and work outward? Focus on helping readers "see" the painting through your eyes.

REVISING Share your description with a friend, and read someone else's. Discuss which details are most vivid and why. Can you replace any unclear words with specific words that clarify your view of the *Mona Lisa*? You may wish to consult a thesaurus to look for new ways to express an idea, but be sure to use a dictionary to check any word you want to use—you need to understand its meaning fully!

PUBLISHING Check your paragraph for errors in grammar, usage, spelling, and punctuation. If you have used any proper adjectives, be sure that you have capitalized them. Then, create an advertisement for the *Mona Lisa,* using your description as the text. Design a brochure or poster that would sell this painting to a museum or art collector.

Extending Your Writing

You may wish to develop this writing exercise into a longer essay. You could write a review of the *Mona Lisa* (or of another work of art) for a school or community newspaper, or an evaluation of the painting for a class in art or history. As you develop your thoughts, you may want to use the library or the Internet to learn more about Leonardo da Vinci's creation of the painting.

Choices: Exploring the Parts of a Sentence

The following activities challenge you to find a connection between the parts of sentences and the world around you. Do the activity below that suits your personality best, and then share your discoveries with your class.

ORGANIZING INFORMATION

In a Nutshell

Compile a one-page listing of the rules in this chapter. Include at least one example for each rule. Then, distribute copies to each of your classmates. Make sure that your page design is easy to use and interesting.

MATHEMATICS

X + Y = Z

Start with ten mathematical equations. Then, translate these equations into sentences and label each subject, verb, and complement. Include examples showing compound subjects, compound verbs, and compound complements.

DEFINING

Where Is Webster When We Need Him?

What do you think of the definition of *sentence*? Try making up a better one! Working with a team, compose several alternative definitions for *sentence*. Then, put your ideas to the test. Present them to your classmates for discussion, and choose the best one.

DIALECT

The Force Is with Him

Hey, *Star Wars* fans, have you ever noticed that Yoda talks rather strangely? Why is that? Check out a *Star Wars* saga book or watch a video of one of the movies that Yoda is in, and write down some of Yoda's speeches. What makes his speech distinctive? What elements of the standard subject-verb-object order does Yoda invert, or reverse? Begin by identifying each subject, verb, and complement (if there is one) of Yoda's sentences. Then, identify the modifiers. Pay special attention to the way he uses *not*. Present your findings to the class.

VISUAL LEARNING

I Did It My Way

Turn to the Diagramming Appendix in your textbook. Do sentence diagrams like the ones there confuse you? No problem—design a new way of visually representing sentence structure. You might use color, shape, position, and even texture if you want. Then, present your new system to your classmates.

VISUAL DEMONSTRATION

Move It!

Help your classmates see how the elements of a sentence can move around. Get a group of five to ten people together, and create a sentence. Begin with a subject, a verb, and a complement. Make giant cards with the simple subject on one card, the verb on another, and the complement on yet another. Then, add other words or word groups—adjectives, adverbs, prepositional phrases, and so on; make cards for those, too. Next, each person should hold up a card and stand in sentence order in front of the class. Then, have some fun! Try different sentence orders—questions, commands, whatever you want. Add and subtract elements. Just move it!

FOREIGN LANGUAGES

Order of the Day

In what order do other languages usually present subjects, verbs, and objects? What differences and similarities can you find between the sentence structures of English and those of, for instance, Spanish? Write a few paragraphs detailing several of these points, or give a demonstration for the class.

Literary Model: Dialogue

Before the mirror, she let the wraps fall from her shoulders to see herself once again in all her glory. Suddenly she gave a cry. The necklace was gone.

Her husband, already half undressed, said, "What's the trouble?"

She turned toward him despairingly, "I . . . I . . . I don't have Mme. Forestier's necklace."

"What! You can't mean it! It's impossible!"

They hunted everywhere, through the folds of the dress, through the folds of the coat, in the pockets. They found nothing.

He asked, "Are you sure you had it when leaving the dance?"

"Yes, I felt it when I was in the hall of the Ministry."

"But if you had lost it on the street, we'd have heard it drop. It must be in the cab."

"Yes, quite likely. Did you get its number?"

"No. Did you notice it, either?"

"No."

They looked at each other aghast. Finally Loisel got dressed again.

"I'll retrace our steps on foot," he said, "to see if I can find it."

—from "The Necklace" by Guy de Maupassant

EXERCISE A

1. What kinds of sentences (*declarative, imperative, interrogative,* or *exclamatory*) does Madame Loisel (the second speaker) use in the passage? ____________________

2. What kinds of sentences does her husband use? ____________________

3. What kinds of sentences does the narrator use? ____________________

4. What kind of sentence do neither the characters nor the narrator use? ____________________

EXERCISE B

1. Compare the kinds of sentences that Madame Loisel and her husband use. How do the different kinds of sentences they use reflect their feelings? ____________________

Literary Model (continued)

2. Why do you think the kinds of sentences Mr. Loisel uses change in the second half of the passage?

EXERCISE C Write a short dialogue in which one character realizes that he or she has lost something and the other character tries to help him or her remember where the item was lost.

EXERCISE D

1. What kinds of sentences did you use in your dialogue?

2. In the dialogue, how did you use sentences of different purposes to show how the characters felt about losing the item and trying to find it?

Writing Application: Summary

We could probably communicate in English with a relatively small group of verbs—*be, do, go, eat, drink, sleep,* and a few others. Think, though, how boring communication would be!

LESS INTERESTING I went to the cafe on the corner and drank a lemonade.

MORE INTERESTING I hightailed it to the cafe on the corner and guzzled down a lemonade.

Fortunately, the English language contains thousands of verbs you can choose from to enliven your writing. Using well-chosen verbs, you, as a writer, can help your reader to visualize what you are describing.

WRITING ACTIVITY

Have you ever decided not to see a movie because you were afraid it would be as boring as the summary of it that you just read? A well-written summary often helps readers decide to view a movie. Think of a movie that impressed you and that you wanted to recommend to everyone you knew. Write a summary of the movie; to keep your writing interesting, be sure to include at least five well-chosen, precise, and lively verbs.

PREWRITING Spend a few minutes remembering the plot and details of the movie and jotting down notes about what you remember. Pay extra attention to those aspects of the movie that first come to your mind, since they are probably what made the movie so memorable and what you will want to emphasize in your summary. Brainstorm for verbs that express the actions portrayed in the movie. In addition, consider the tone you will adopt. For instance, do you want to sound casual or formal?

WRITING Decide how you will structure your summary. Will you arrange your ideas in some order other than chronological? If other ideas or details occur to you as you write, add them.

REVISING Examine your draft to determine whether you can replace some of the verbs with others that are more precise or lively. A thesaurus can help you with this step, but double-check a dictionary to make sure that a word suggested by the thesaurus is appropriate for the sentence. Try out your draft on a friend to see whether your summary makes him or her want to see the movie.

PUBLISHING Check your summary for errors in grammar, usage, punctuation, and spelling. Make sure you have followed capitalization and punctuation rules for movie titles. Consider submitting your summary for publication in your school newspaper or on a Web site concerned with movies. Find out submission dates and what the guidelines are for length.

EXTENDING YOUR WRITING

You may want to develop this writing activity further. You could write a review of the movie and include part or all of your summary in the review. Submit your piece to a newspaper, magazine, or Web site that publishes movie reviews.

Choices: Examining Phrases

The following activities challenge you to find a connection between phrases and the world around you. Do the activity below that suits your personality best, and then share your discoveries with your class.

MUSIC

Do Re Mi

Musicians use phrases. If you are a musician, tell the class what a musical phrase is. Be sure to play some examples. Then, create a chart that shows how grammatical phrases and musical phrases are used in similar ways. Use at least three examples to demonstrate the similarities.

HISTORICAL RESEARCH

Attila the Hun

Throughout history, there have been people who were known by their names and an appositive. Attila the Hun is one. Gather as many of these names as you can find. You should be able to find at least five, but try to come up with as many as ten. Then, using appositives, write a very short biography for each person. Be sure to point out which names use commas with their appositives and which do not.

CREATIVE WRITING

You, Wonderful You

If someone were writing about you twenty-five years from now, what appositives might be used? Be that someone. Write at least twenty sentences that use appositives (for the future you, of course). Include some short appositives and some quite long ones.

GAMES

Game Show Host

Divide the class into groups. Have each group brainstorm participles and some nouns that they commonly modify, such as *burnt toast, greased lightning,* and *roasted peanuts*. At the end of two minutes, collect each list. Then, write each participle and noun on the board, and answer any objections to the pairings. Eliminate any that are impossible or illogical. The team with the most participles modifying nouns wins!

WRITING

Mission Possible

If you've got a purpose and somebody asks you what it is, chances are you'll use an infinitive or two to answer the question. Working with your classmates, use infinitives to write five possible mission statements for the class. Then, with your teacher's permission, post your statements in your classroom.

RESEARCH

In the Pink

Phrases play a big role in idioms. Idioms like *in hot water, wearing your heart on your sleeve,* and *reading between the lines* can make people who aren't familiar with them frown and scratch their heads. However, they do make more sense if you know the story behind them. Start by brainstorming a list of at least ten idioms that are phrases or that contain phrases. Then, research the stories behind a few of these phrases. Report your findings to the class.

ART

Running Shoes

If you like a joke and you can draw, try this project. Illustrate at least five expressions that use participles and that conjure up humorous images, such as a *walking stick,* or *baked Alaska*. Then, display your images, but without the participial phrase. Let your classmates write their guesses at the bottom of each picture.

ORIGINAL PROJECTS

It's up to You

You have good ideas. Pick one, and create your own project. Use infinitives to write a list of your lifetime goals. Make a list of participles used in cooking. Compose a list of gerunds used in careers or sports. Whatever you decide to do, be sure to get your teacher's approval before you start.

Literary Model: Description

In a forest of mixed growth somewhere on the eastern spurs of the Carpathians, a man stood one winter night watching and listening, as though he waited for some beast of the woods to come within the range of his vision and, later, of his rifle. But the game for whose presence he kept so keen an outlook was none that figured in the sportsman's calendar as lawful and proper for the chase; Ulrich von Gradwitz patrolled the dark forest in quest of a human enemy.

—from "The Interlopers" by Saki

EXERCISE A In the above paragraph, identify each underlined prepositional phrase as an *adverb* phrase or an *adjective* phrase and give the word that each phrase modifies. The first prepositional phrase has been identified for you as an example.

1. *In a forest—adverb—stood* **5.** ______ **9.** ______

2. ______ **6.** ______ **10.** ______

3. ______ **7.** ______ **11.** ______

4. ______ **8.** ______

EXERCISE B

1. Rewrite the last three lines of the text without any of the prepositional phrases.

______

______

______

______

2. Is the paragraph easier or more difficult to understand without the phrases? What kind of information is missing without them?

______

______

______

Literary Model (continued)

EXERCISE C Rewrite the paragraph, replacing each of the prepositional phrases you identified in Exercise A with a prepositional phrase of your own invention. Your phrases may modify different words but should function in the same way as the originals (as either adjective or adverb phrases). Feel free to change any other words so that your new phrases make sense.

EXERCISE D

1. Did your phrases change the setting and tone of the original passage? If so, how? If not, could the setting and tone have been changed if you had used other phrases?

2. Consider what adverb phrases tell about the words they modify. Why did changing the adverb phrases affect the setting of the original passage?

Writing Application: Speech

A subject and predicate that agree and express a complete thought make up the bare bones of a sentence. To add details, writers often use prepositional phrases.

LESS SPECIFIC People have not always known about dinosaurs.

MORE SPECIFIC Before the 1822 discovery of a giant fossilized tooth by Mary Ann Mantell in England, people did not know about dinosaurs. The giant reptiles were not given the name of "terrible lizard" by Richard Owen until 1841.

Eight prepositional phrases in the second and third sentences tell how, when, and where people first became aware of the dinosaur fossil record.

Writing Activity

You have volunteered to accompany a class of fourth-graders on their field trip to your city's museum of natural history. For fourth-graders, the highlight of the field trip will be visiting the fossil exhibit. Prepare a five-minute speech to tell the children about fossils. Use prepositional phrases to add details to your speech.

PREWRITING Consult print reference sources, the Internet, or both to learn about the discovery of the fossil record. (Two facts to get you started appear in the example above.) Take notes on what you find, picking out the facts that are most basic to the children's understanding and that fourth-graders will find most interesting. Think of times when you have enjoyed listening to speakers. How did they keep your attention?

WRITING Write your presentation, organizing the information so it is easy to follow. Remember, because you are speaking to fourth-graders, you will have to choose words that they will understand.

REVISING Read your presentation aloud slowly and clearly to several people, and ask them to take brief notes. Then, look at their notes—did they list all of your main points? If not, you may need to emphasize those points more in your presentation.

PUBLISHING Even though your audience will not see your written product, check it for spelling and punctuation errors that may trip you up while reading it aloud. Read your presentation to your class, using the classroom as an imaginary museum.

Extending Your Writing

You may wish to develop this writing exercise further. Schools and museums welcome volunteer efforts. You could expand your research and presentation into a script for museum guides, or you could add illustrations and create a booklet for a museum to give to students on field trips to the museum.

NAME CLASS DATE

Choices: Exploring Clauses

The following activities challenge you to find a connection between clauses and the world around you. Do the activity below that suits your personality best, and then share your discoveries with your class.

MUSIC

If I Had the Wings of an Angel

Subordinating conjunctions begin many popular songs. Compile a list of opening lines that begin with a subordinating conjunction, and post the list in the classroom. Be sure to underline each subordinate clause and highlight each subordinating conjunction.

REPRESENTING

Around and Around We Go

Show your classmates how adverb clauses can often be moved from the end of a sentence to the beginning or vice versa. Write a sentence that includes two parts: an independent clause and an adverb clause. Using all lowercase letters and no punctuation, write or print out several copies of each clause. Cut out each clause so it is on its own strip of paper. Then, tape the strips together, alternating your two clauses. Ta-da! You have an endless statement that makes sense, no matter which clause comes first. Give two copies of each clause to your classmates, and ask them to capitalize and punctuate both possible versions of the sentence.

DRAMA

He Said, She Said

Write a dialogue between two people who are deciding where to go on Saturday night. One speaks only in independent clauses; the other speaks only in subordinate clauses. Record your dialogue on video, or perform it for the class.

MATHEMATICS

One Times One Plus One

Forge a connection between mathematical clauses and grammatical clauses. Plan and conduct a short seminar in mathematical clauses. Begin with an independent clause—a simple equation. Then, add parenthetical expressions that make the equation more complex.

PERFORMANCE

Start a Chain Reaction

Try this project if you like surprises! First, make sure everyone in the class has a list of subordinating conjunctions and relative pronouns. Then, you start the ball rolling by giving one classmate an independent clause. He or she adds on a subordinate clause and passes on the sentence to the next person. When the last person adds a clause, you'll have an incredibly long sentence that will probably be a very strange and funny story. You can do this project aloud or by passing around a sheet of paper. If you do the project on paper, be sure to read the story to the class.

REPRESENTING

Decisions, Decisions

Make a flowchart showing the process of deciding whether a word group is a phrase or an independent or a subordinate clause. Naturally, you'll have steps for finding the subject and the verb. You'll want a step for determining whether the word group is a complete thought, too. Neatly transfer your flowchart to poster board. Feel free to jazz up your chart with colors and designs.

ORIGINAL PROJECTS

Have It Your Way

Create a project of your own. Write and teach a marching song about clauses to the class. Write a monologue composed only of subordinate clauses, such as *If only I had. . . .* Look up the etymology and definitions of the word *clause,* and report what you learn. Find out what the legal term *clause* means. Color-code the adverb and adjective clauses in a page of writing. Cut up some complex sentences into clauses, and ask your classmates to put them back together. Be sure to get your teacher's approval before starting your project.

Literary Model: Poetry

When I heard the learn'd astronomer,
When the proofs, the figures, were ranged in columns before me,
When I was shown the charts and diagrams, to add, divide, and measure them,
When I sitting heard the astronomer where he lectured with much applause in
the lecture room,
How soon unaccountable I became tired and sick,
Till rising and gliding out I wandered off by myself,
In the mystical moist night air, and from time to time,
Looked up in perfect silence at the stars.

—"When I Heard the Learn'd Astronomer" by Walt Whitman

EXERCISE A

1. On the lines below, write the subject and verb of each clause in the poem. Next to the subject and verb, write *S* if the clause is subordinate or *I* if the clause is independent. One clause from the last four lines has been indentified for you.

   I wandered, looked—S

2. It may surprise you to realize that the poem is one long sentence. Based on the clauses you identified in Item 1, what kind of sentence is it: simple, compound, complex, or compound-complex?

EXERCISE B As you can see, the poem begins with a series of increasingly longer clauses. How might the length and number of these clauses indicate how the speaker feels about the astronomer's lecture?

Literary Model (continued)

EXERCISE C Write a short poem describing a lecture or a speech you once heard and how you felt about it. Make your poem one long sentence as Whitman did.

EXERCISE D

1. On the lines below, write the subject and verb of each clause you used in your poem. Next to the subject and verb, write *S* if the clause is subordinate or *I* if the clause is independent.

2. What kind of sentence is your poem: simple, compound, complex, or compound-complex?

3. Explain how your use of clauses helps describe the lecture or speech. For instance, did you use subordinate clauses for less important ideas and independent clauses for more important ones? Did you use long or short clauses to help express your meaning? Explain your answers.

Writing Application: Instructions

Characteristics such as age and level of experience influence a person's ability to understand a set of instructions. For example, a teenager who has been cooking and creating recipes since the age of seven will probably find it easier to understand instructions for how to make lasagna than another teenager whose cooking experience consists of heating a frozen dinner in a microwave oven. The writing used in the instructions given to the beginner should contain more simple sentences and fewer compound, complex, and compound-complex sentences.

SIMPLE Let eggs reach room temperature. Beat four eggs for one minute. Add them to the batter.

COMPOUND-COMPLEX Beat for one minute four eggs that have reached room temperature; then, add them to the batter.

In any kind of writing—but especially in informative pieces of writing—consider your audience when you choose sentence structures.

Writing Activity

Think of something that you know how to do or make that would be appropriate for both children and adults. Write two sets of instructions for your activity: one that a group of second-grade students can follow without any difficulty, and the other that a group of adults can successfully follow. Be sure to tailor your choice of sentence structures according to the audience.

PREWRITING Use a flowchart or some other type of diagram to list all the steps and materials that need to be included in your instructions. Then, while visualizing yourself actually performing the task, check that you have included every step and material in the diagram.

WRITING Use what you have written in your diagram to guide you as you write a draft of each set of instructions. Remember to choose sentence structures according to whether the instructions are intended for the second-grade students or the adults. You should use mostly simple sentences in your instructions for the children.

REVISING Read your two drafts to two classmates to see whether they can tell which set of instructions is intended for which audience. If it is not completely obvious, then you need to revise sentence structures. You will also need to make sure your vocabulary is appropriate for each audience. If your classmates are not familiar with your topic, ask them whether they think the instructions are clear enough.

PUBLISHING Put your two sets of instructions aside for a while, then proofread them slowly later. Check that all your sentences are complete sentences and that you have correctly used punctuation in your compound, complex, and compound-complex sentences. Proofread for other errors in grammar, usage, spelling, and punctuation. Then, use one set of instructions to demonstrate the steps of your activity to the class.

Extending Your Writing

Along with one or two of your classmates, turn your instructions into a handy guidebook. First, your group needs to determine the audience of your guidebook: adults, children, or a combination of the two. Write a brief but helpful introduction that explains the content of your guide. Decide which instructions to include, come up with the best way to bind them together, and illustrate the pages and cover of your book.

Choices: Exploring Agreement

The following activities challenge you to find a connection between subject-verb agreement and pronoun-antecedent agreement and the world around you. Do the activity below that suits your personality best, and then share your discoveries with your class.

BUILDING BACKGROUND KNOWLEDGE

Rock-and-Roll

There are quite a number of pairs of nouns that go together. They actually name only one thing. These pairs are called *binomials*. Get together with a friend and brainstorm a list of binomials. You could start with *macaroni and cheese* or *horse and carriage*. When you're done, pass out copies of your list for your classmates to insert in their English notebooks.

GRAPHICS

Neither Fish nor Fowl

Some indefinite pronouns really are indefinite; they can be singular or plural. You know the ones—*all, any, more, most, none,* and *some*. Design a poster to show your classmates. Choose five indefinite pronouns that can be singular or plural. For each pronoun, write two sentences: one for each context.

FOREIGN LANGUAGES

¿Habla Español?

Interview a few people who speak or are learning a foreign language. Find out if other languages require subjects and verbs to agree. Make a handout of examples for your classmates, and report back to the class.

CONTEST

STOP!

Record a dialogue or monologue. Sprinkle subject-verb errors and pronoun-antecedent agreement errors throughout. Then, divide the class into two teams. Play your recording. When someone hears an error, he or she yells "STOP!" Stop and ask the person to correct the error. Proper corrections earn a point. Incorrect stops lose a point. The team with the most points wins.

MATHEMATICS

The Latest Statistics

Some people say that we live in the age of statistics. Studies, statistical analyses, and polls on every possible subject are being made daily. Pick one recent statistical analysis. (They're in newspapers all the time.) Study it and write out some of the facts that the study found. Be sure to use percentages and fractions as subjects and antecedents. Then, report on the topic, and give your classmates a chance to hear how percentages and fractions sound when they agree with verbs and antecedents.

DRAMA

Collective Decisions

Sometimes deciding whether collective nouns are singular or plural is easy, and sometimes it's not. Make it easy for your classmates. In a group, act out a few situations. First, write a half-dozen sentences, each of which is a scenario that your group acts out. Write three in which the group acts as a unit and three in which the group members act individually. Make sure you write the sentence that you are acting out on the board.

ORIGINAL PROJECTS

Blaze Your Own Trail

There are plenty of lists you could compile for this chapter—lists of plural nouns that actually are singular, plural nouns *(pants)* that name only one thing, titles that are plural *(Wuthering Heights)*, and many more. Compile one of these lists or come up with your own activity. Go on a scavenger hunt for agreement errors in magazines and newspapers. Write a riddle or a limerick. Design a brochure. Perform a comedy routine. If you want to do something new, do it! Just make sure your activity relates to agreement.

Proofreading Application: Report

Good writers are generally good proofreaders. Readers tend to admire and trust writing that is error-free. Make sure that you correct all errors in grammar, usage, spelling, and punctuation in your writing. Your readers will have more confidence in your words if you have done your best to proofread carefully.

Journalists aren't the only people who write reports. Many jobs require daily reports as well as monthly and quarterly reports. Very likely, you will write reports when you enter the workforce as an adult.

When you write reports, make sure that you proofread carefully for agreement. Your subjects and verbs or pronouns and antecedents must agree. Otherwise, you will not be able to convey accurate information. For instance, if you use a singular subject with a plural verb, your readers will think that something has been left out. Consequently, they will question the accuracy of your facts.

Proofreading Activity

In the following report, find and correct the agreement errors. Use proofreading symbols such as those on page 935 of *Elements of Language* to make your corrections.

Example Since September, the goal of the school beautification committee ~~have~~ *has* been to create a garden.

That garden, thanks to the help of many people, are almost completed. Many businesses in our town is to be thanked for their contribution to this project. For example, Garden Furnishings promise to deliver a beautiful concrete bench this week.

Amber O'Hara and Franklin Gibson worked hard on her and his spectacular design for the garden. Everybody on the committee has given their free time to create fifty custom stepping stones for a walkway. The mosaics of broken tile that decorate each stone is especially appreciated because the design incorporates our school mascot.

Three myrtle trees and a young maple is still needed to shade the area. Trees Galore have agreed to donate whatever we need for our project. Don't anyone know where we can get the free truckload of gravel that we still need? The grand opening of the ninth grade's contribution to the school grounds are scheduled for March 17.

Literary Model: Poetry

Because I could not stop for Death
By Emily Dickinson

Because I could not stop for Death—
He kindly stopped for me—
The Carriage held but just Ourselves—
And Immortality.

We slowly drove—He knew no haste
And I had put away
My labor and my leisure too,
For His Civility—

We passed the School, where Children strove
At Recess—in the Ring—
We passed the Fields of Gazing Grain—
We passed the Setting Sun—

Or rather—He passed Us—
The Dews drew quivering and chill—
For only Gossamer, my Gown—
My Tippet—only Tulle—

We paused before a House that seemed
A Swelling of the Ground—
The Roof was scarcely visible—
The Cornice—in the Ground—

Since then—'tis Centuries—and yet
Feels shorter than the Day
I first surmised the Horses Heads
Were toward Eternity—

EXERCISE A Name the two pronouns that refer exclusively to Death in the above poem.

____

EXERCISE B

1. When an antecedent is an abstract noun, generally the neuter third-person singular pronouns *it* and *its* are used to refer to it. Why do you think Emily Dickinson chose to use pronouns that indicate masculine gender to refer to Death?

____

____

2. If Dickinson had indicated, through the use of pronouns, that Death had a feminine persona, how might the poem have been different?

____

Literary Model (continued)

EXERCISE C The subject of Dickinson's poem is the abstract quality or idea of Death. Think of a different quality or idea—for example, beauty, truth, strength, or goodness—and write a poem that has this idea as the poem's subject. Determine whether the persona of the quality or idea you have chosen is masculine or feminine, and use the appropriate pronouns when referring to it.

EXERCISE D Analyze your choice of gender for the persona of the quality or idea that is the subject of your poem.

Writing Application: Report

Language is never static. Although changes in a language happen slowly, they do occur. For instance, nowadays in informal conversation you'll often hear plural personal pronouns being used to refer to singular antecedents that can be either masculine or feminine. That is, it's not uncommon to hear "Everyone at that table is wearing *their* letter jacket." This usage might have been totally unacceptable to a nineteenth-century English grammarian. Yet such usage is gradually becoming more common in writing, and someday it may become acceptable as standard written English. For the present, though, you should avoid this and all other instances of nonstandard usage in formal writing and speaking, including those instances related to subject-verb agreement.

NONSTANDARD Neither of us like big trucks.

STANDARD Neither of us likes big trucks.

WRITING ACTIVITY

How much does a person's favorite type of vehicle reveal about his or her personality? It might reveal nothing at all—but it can be a fun topic to explore. Poll several friends or classmates about their favorite vehicles, and write a paragraph describing the results and your interpretation of the survey.

PREWRITING Ask four to six friends or classmates which three adjectives best describe their personalities and what their favorite types of vehicles are. Record this information on a chart that you have prepared prior to beginning your survey. Classifying responses by means of the chart will help you write your paragraph logically. After completing the survey, think about the tone you want your writing to have.

WRITING Using the information in your chart, write your draft freely, yet at the same time try to express your ideas clearly. Analyze your survey results to determine the topic sentence for your paragraph.

REVISING Read your paragraph several times, first concentrating on content, then on organization, and finally on style. Make sure that your topic sentence is adequately supported by details. Ask yourself if the writing will hold the attention of your reader.

PUBLISHING Identify the subject(s) and verb(s) in each sentence, and check for any errors in subject-verb agreement. Also, check for other errors in usage and mechanics. Be sure you have capitalized all proper nouns. Create a chart as a visual aid to accompany your report. Publish your report and chart and, with your teacher's permission, post it on the board or on your class Web site.

EXTENDING YOUR WRITING

You may wish to conduct a more extensive survey and then develop this writing exercise into a longer essay. Do an Internet search for online publications of student writing, and submit your essay.

NAME CLASS DATE

Choices: Investigating Verbs

The following activities challenge you to find a connection between sentences and the world around you. Do the activity below that suits your personality best, and then share your discoveries with your class.

LINGUISTICS

Strike Out!

Some verbs have more than one past or past participle form, although the forms are not always interchangeable. The past participle of *strike,* for example, may be *struck* or *stricken*. Get together with several friends and research a list of other verbs that have alternative past or past participle forms. Then, prepare a handout for your classmates that includes the verbs, the alternative forms, and example sentences using the alternatives if they have different meanings.

DISCUSSION

Yo!

The way people talk with their friends on a relaxed Sunday afternoon is often quite different from the way they talk at the office or in school bright and early Monday morning. Why does this difference exist? What purpose does it serve? How might a listener react to informal speech in a formal situation? How might a listener react to formal speech in an informal situation? Lead a discussion of these and related questions.

VIDEO

Three of a Kind

Be a movie star! Working with two friends, write and videotape a dialogue among three people. One person speaks only in the present tense, one speaks only in the past tense, and the other speaks only in the future tense. Before you begin writing, talk about the kind of outlook on life that each of these three characters might have. Ask yourself how they might come into conflict. Then, videotape your dialogue. When you've finished taping, show your video to the class. Then, sit back and bask in the applause!

ART

A Work in Progress

Illustrate several different stages of an event to help you and your classmates understand how the tenses are used. You could use a paint program on a computer or draw the pictures by hand. Under each picture, write a sentence describing the action, underline the verb, and label its tense.

STUDY AIDS

Fuel Injection

Some people remember the different tenses easily, but others may need a way to speed up the process. Write a poem or rap, or devise some other kind of study aid to help your classmates master these tenses. Begin by writing down and studying the rules for each tense. When you've got your study aid ready, share it with your class.

ART

The Setting Sun

Create small posters illustrating the proper use of the troublesome verbs *lie/lay, sit/set,* and *rise/raise.* For instance, you could find or draw pictures of the sun setting and rising. If you want to go hog-wild, you could design a deck of playing cards, with each card illustrating a situation in which one of these verbs is used correctly. Naturally, you will need to include a sentence that each picture illustrates.

ORIGINAL PROJECT

Made to Order

Create your own project. Speak using archaic or obsolete verbs for a day, and dress the part. Better yet, put on a play in which modern English speakers go through a time warp and meet English speakers from earlier times and hear the way they *spake,* not *spoke.* Poll English teachers for their opinions on the most misused verbs and brainstorm ways to improve usage. What will you do? Whatever you decide, be sure to get your teacher's approval first.

Proofreading Application: Letter

Good writers generally are good proofreaders. Learn to become a careful proofreader so that you can correct errors in grammar, usage, spelling, and punctuation. Readers will have more trust in what you're communicating if you do your best to make sure that your writing is error-free.

Many times in your life, you will want or need to write about past events. For instance, you might write a letter to a friend and tell about the things that have happened. You may write about your work experiences for an application. Or you may need to write a report at work when you are older.

Whenever you write about past events, be particularly careful about using correct verb forms and tenses. Correct verb forms allow readers to focus on the meaning of your writing. Was the first event over before the second one began? Is the first event still going on? What is happening now? Don't leave these questions in your readers' minds. Proofread your verbs carefully.

Proofreading Activity

In the following excerpt from a letter of application, correct the errors in verb form and tense. Use proofreading symbols such as those on page 935 of *Elements of Language* to make your corrections.

Example My skills and interest in engineering ~~makes~~ *make* me an ideal candidate for your summer program in engineering.

I wanted to be an engineer before I had known what engineers are. When I had been only five years old, I builded a system of roads and waterways in my backyard. The system included waterwheels and, later, a lock for the canal to the "lake" that I created. My mother has took pictures of many of my projects, and I am enclosing copies of these photographs. As I had grown, I moved on to metal and plastic models, and those with moving parts always were my favorites. Eventually, I begun to design my own animated models. I have maked cranes, conveyor belts, pistons, merry-go-rounds, and many other structures. My father has teached me basic computer programming, which I had used to direct several robots.

I always show up on time, worked hard, and set my standards high. Please consider me for your upcoming summer session.

NAME CLASS DATE

Literary Model: Narration

On December the third, the wind changed overnight, and it was winter. Until then the autumn had been mellow, soft. The leaves had lingered on the trees, golden-red, and the hedgerows were still green. The earth was rich where the plow had turned it.

Nat Hocken, because of a wartime disability, had a pension and did not work full time at the farm. He worked three days a week, and they gave him the lighter jobs: hedging, thatching, repairs to the farm buildings.

—from "The Birds" by Daphne du Maurier

EXERCISE A Underline the verbs in the passage above.

EXERCISE B

1. In the list below, circle each verb tense that is used in the passage.

present tense	past tense	future tense
present perfect tense	past perfect tense	future perfect tense

2. Why does the author need to use more than one verb tense in the passage?

3. In the first paragraph, what two words signal that the verb tense is about to change?

Literary Model (continued)

EXERCISE C Have you ever suddenly realized that what is happening to you at the present moment had been foreshadowed by events in the past? Perhaps a roomful of people have just shouted "Surprise!" at you, and you realize that last week when you thought your best friend was avoiding you, she actually had been planning your surprise party. Using an experience like this one or an event that you make up, write a passage in which you use at least two verb tenses to narrate an event.

EXERCISE D

1. Which verb tenses did you use in your passage?

2. Did you use words or phrases to signal that the tense was about to change? If so, what are they? If not, what are some words or phrases you could have used?

3. Why is it sometimes more effective to use a change in verb tense, such as in a flashback, than it is to tell a story or event in strict chronological order?

Writing Application: Personal Essay

Events in personal essays, just as in real life, can happen in the past, present, or future. In English the tense of the verb indicates the time of the action or of the state of being that the verb is expressing. You, as a writer, can help your reader understand when the events in a personal essay take place by using verb tense correctly. Sometimes you will need to use different tenses in a paragraph or even in the same sentence.

EXAMPLE The house had not been wired to code, and the inevitable result was that it caught on fire and was completely destroyed. Whatever will become of the unfortunate family who lived next door?

You can also help your reader understand the timing of events in your personal essay by not changing needlessly from one tense to another.

INCONSISTENT TENSE The house catches on fire. The firefighters quickly arrived.

CONSISTENT TENSE The house **caught** on fire. The firefighters quickly **arrived.**

Writing Activity

What is a hobby, sport, or other activity that you presently enjoy doing and have enjoyed doing for several years? Think back to when you first started doing this activity. Then, consider why you have continued to do it over a period of time. Write a personal essay in which you describe what your initial experience with the activity was like; whether your appreciation of the activity has grown and, if so, how; and what you expect your relationship to the activity to be like as you grow older. Use at least four different verb tenses in your essay.

PREWRITING Use a clustering or webbing technique to break your topic down into smaller parts. Consider having the following radiate from the central topic circle: one cluster of ideas that deals with your initial experience with the activity, another cluster dealing with your present relationship to it, and a third cluster that deals with your future relationship to it. Before you begin writing your draft, determine who your audience will be.

WRITING Using the information in the cluster diagram, write your draft freely, without concentrating too much on errors in grammar, usage, spelling, and punctuation. Ask yourself whether chronological order is the best way to arrange your ideas.

REVISING Have a classmate read your draft. Ask him or her to tell you its strengths and weaknesses, as well as a few suggestions for improving it. In an effort to make your writing as focused as possible, make sure your draft is not repetitive or wordy.

PUBLISHING Check that you have used at least four verb tenses, that they are all used correctly, and that you have not used tenses inconsistently. Use a dictionary or your textbook to verify the spelling of irregular verb forms. Then, share your essay with someone else who leads or participates in this activity.

Extending Your Writing

Are there any newsletters or magazines that publish articles on the kind of hobby, sport, or other activity that you wrote about? Revise your essay to appeal to that publication's audience, and submit your essay for publication.

Choices: Investigating Pronouns

The following activities challenge you to find a connection between pronoun usage and the world around you. Do the activity below that suits your personality best, and then share your discoveries with your class.

HISTORY

Junkyard or Antique Shop?

Whatever happened to those old-fashioned *thee*'s and *thou*'s? They wound up in the junkyard of English. There can be a lot of good stuff at a junkyard, though. Writers can make poetry out of such out-of-date words. Make a poster titled "Language Junkyard" or "Antique Shop of English." On it, write words and expressions that are no longer used or that are no longer considered standard. Don't limit yourself to pronouns. Anything goes. With your teacher's permission, hang your poster in the hall.

SURVEY

The Hit Parade

With permission, record conversations. Then, count the number of personal pronouns used. Which personal pronoun is used the most often in your experiment? Which ones are most often used incorrectly? Which ones are most often used correctly? Present the class with an ordered listing of your results. Present, too, your opinions about the results you obtained.

FOREIGN LANGUAGES

Él y Ella

How do other languages handle pronouns? Do other languages have nominative, objective, and possessive cases? What about second- and third-person singular and plural? How are these handled in, say, Spanish? Find out, and share your finding with your classmates.

BUILDING BACKGROUND KNOWLEDGE

Close Relatives

Look up the word *nominative*. What is its root word? Then, brainstorm as many words as you can that share this same root word. Use each of these words in a sentence. Next, create a poster. Write the root word in the center, and create a chart showing how each word relates to the root word.

RESEARCH

Street Lingo

Standard English does not have a special pronoun for second-person plural. However, nonstandard varieties of English do. In fact, there are several. List some expressions that include these special pronouns. In what geographical region or regions are they used? Let your classmates know the answers to these questions.

CONVERSATION

Dialogue

What would conversations sound like if people used *whom* as often as standard usage requires? Write a ten-line dialogue that involves one person who always uses *who* and another person who always uses *whom*. As you alternate from one speaker to the other, make sure to use *who* or *whom* correctly at least once in each line of conversation.

WRITING

Travel Article

Just how important are pronouns, anyway? Find out by trying to write a few paragraphs without using any pronouns. Pretend you are a travel writer whose assignment is to describe a trip you have taken with your friends or family. Give detailed descriptions of the scenery, activities, and people you encountered. Don't hold back, but remember—absolutely no pronouns allowed!

ART

In Black and White

Elliptical clauses can be tricky. Take, for instance, *He liked the movie more than her.* Does this sentence mean that she didn't like the movie as much as he did or that he liked the movie more than he liked her? Find or create a few of these confusing sentences. Then, draw cartoons illustrating the situations that the sentences describe. Don't forget to include the unintended results!

Proofreading Application: Speech

Good writers are generally good proofreaders. Readers tend to admire and trust writing that is error-free. Make sure that you correct all errors in grammar, usage, spelling, and punctuation in your writing. Your readers will have more confidence in your words if you have done your best to proofread carefully.

Throughout your school and work careers, you will make speeches. Pronoun errors in speeches are particularly troublesome because listeners cannot go back and listen to the speech again. Whether your speech is short or long, take special care to proofread for correct pronoun case and references. Correct pronoun usage ensures that your ideas will get the hearing they deserve.

Proofreading Activity

In the following speech, find any errors in pronoun use and correct them. Use proofreading symbols such as those on page 935 of *Elements of Language* to make your corrections. You may need to rewrite some of the sentences.

Example Is Mr. Valdez the teacher ~~whom~~ who is retiring?

As most of you know, Mr. Valdez is retiring this year. When Mrs. Adams asked me if I would give a speech about he and his work, I was honored. I have heard nothing but kindhearted comments about Mr. Valdez, no matter who I have asked. He has given mine fellow students and I more than respect; he has given us hope for the future. In our school yearbooks over the past twenty years, they show dozens of pictures of Mr. Valdez surrounded by a crowd of admiring students.

The photographs reminded me, as they would remind any of we students, of many lively scenes from Mr. Valdez's class. I will never forget the day Principal Huffman came to Mr. Valdez's classroom to announce that he'd won the district's Educator of the Year award. Those of you whom are seniors can remember the countless hours that Mr. Valdez has spent listening to problems and helping we to understand mathematics. Because we had the chance to experience the humor and inspiration of Mr. Valdez, you and me are extremely lucky. Thank you, Mr. Valdez.

Literary Model: Poetry

The Secret
by Denise Levertov

Two girls discover
the secret of life
in a sudden line of
poetry.

I who don't know the
secret write
the line. They
told me

(through a third person)
they had found it
but not what it was
not even

what line it was. No doubt
by now, more than a week
later, they have forgotten
the secret,
the line, the name of
the poem. I love them for
finding what
I can't find,
and for loving me
for the line I wrote,
and for forgetting it
so that
a thousand times, till death
finds them, they may
discover it again, in other
lines

in other
happenings. And for
wanting to know it,
for
assuming there is
such a secret, yes,
for that
most of all.

EXERCISE A

1. To whom do the pronouns *I* and *me* refer in the poem?

2. What is the antecedent of the pronouns *they* and *them?*

3. To what antecedents does the pronoun *it* refer at different points in the poem?

EXERCISE B

1. What is the effect of using *it* throughout the poem to refer to different antecedents at different times?

2. How might the ambiguity over what *it* refers to relate to the theme and title of the poem?

Literary Model (continued)

EXERCISE C Write a short poem about a secret or a mystery. Experiment with using ambiguous pronoun references to heighten the sense of not knowing what the secret or mystery is.

EXERCISE D

1. What kinds of unclear pronoun references did you use, and why are they unclear?

2. How did your use of ambiguous pronoun references contribute to the theme of your poem?

3. How would your poem be different if you revised it to avoid the ambiguous pronouns?

Writing Application: Biographical Sketch

What would we do without pronouns? For one thing, we would be making statements like this: *Marsha prefers to stay in Marsha's room, but Marsha's mom wants Marsha and Marsha's sister Samantha to spend more time with the family.* Since pronouns take the place of nouns, they can eliminate instances of repetition. However, when you use pronouns in your writing, you should help out your readers by not using too many of them and by making sure that each one you use refers clearly to its antecedent.

CONFUSING Marsha brought Samantha some flowers. As she walked through the kitchen, she smelled and admired them. They were very pretty.

CLEAR Marsha brought Samantha some flowers. As Marsha walked through the kitchen, she smelled and admired the bouquet. The daffodils in particular were very pretty.

Writing Activity

Which historical figure do you most admire? The person who first comes to your mind must have done so for some good reasons—considering how many historical figures you've learned about over the years. Write a biographical sketch or short essay about this person. Use a variety of pronouns (at least eight of them) as subjects, predicate nominatives, direct and indirect objects, and objects of prepositions.

PREWRITING Consider using a time line to organize information chronologically. Since you are writing a biographical sketch or short essay, you will need to focus on a limited number of events in the person's life—preferably those that have the most significance for you. Then, increase your readers' interest level in your writing by including many attention-holding details about each event. Consult print and online encyclopedias and other reference materials to discover additional information about the person.

WRITING After you have written an introductory paragraph, use each event as the topic sentence of a paragraph. Support the topic sentence with the details you already knew and those you learned in reference materials. Make sure that your admiration for the person is evident in your writing.

REVISING After you have finished your draft, leave it alone for a while; then, read it aloud to yourself. Reading aloud may help you notice rough spots that could be improved. Replace any weak words with more precise ones.

PUBLISHING Check that at least eight pronouns appear in your sketch or essay and that they are used in different positions. Be sure that each one is in the correct case and refers clearly to its antecedent. Also, check your essay for errors in spelling and punctuation. With your teacher's permission, post your essay in the classroom.

Extending Your Writing

You might develop this writing exercise into a longer biographical essay. Then you could collect your classmates' essays and, adding your own, create an anthology. The anthology could be presented to a middle school or elementary school library.

Choices: Exploring Modifiers

The following activities challenge you to find a connection between modifiers and the world around you. Do the activity below that suits your personality best, and then share your discoveries with your class.

VISUAL

Go with the Flow

Sometimes a picture makes everything clear. If identifying adverbs and adjectives is easy for you, consider this project. Make a flow chart detailing the steps in identifying a modifier as an adjective or an adverb. With your teacher's permission, hang your chart in the classroom.

BUILDING BACKGROUND KNOWLEDGE

There's Always an Exception

Some adverbs do not end in *–ly*. For instance, we don't say, "He ran fastly." Can you think of other adverbs that don't end in *–ly*? Brainstorm a list of these adverbs, use each one correctly in a sentence, and give everybody in the class a handout for their notebooks.

CONTEST

Just for Laughs

Misplaced modifiers are often funny, even though the writer may not have intended readers to laugh. Hold a contest to see who can write (and correct) the most hilarious misplaced modifier. You'll need a panel of judges. Make sure the winner's entry receives an award.

GROUP DEMONSTRATION

Human Flashcards

Don't worry, shy people, these are nonspeaking parts. Take one or two sentences containing one-word modifiers such as *only, just,* and *even* and prepare large flashcards for each word in the sentences. Make a special card for the one-word modifiers, perhaps using a red, not black, marker. One person holds each card, and everyone stands in sentence order in front of the class. Then, the spotlight falls on the person with the one-word modifier card. He or she gets to move around, creating different meanings and some rather strange errors.

WORD ASSOCIATION

The Best of the Best

Everybody has an opinion. Find out what your classmates' thoughts are on these topics: movies, books, fictional characters, and places to visit. Create a list of superlatives such as *funniest, coldest, happiest, most impressive,* or *most memorable.* Get into groups of four or fewer, and have each group member share his or her own idea of the most memorable place to visit, funniest movie, and so on.

WRITING

"I Before E . . ."

Do you remember that old rhyme, "*I* before *e* except after *c* . . ." It was and is a big help in spelling. Write a similar rhyme for comparisons, one that will help your classmates remember when to use the comparative form and when to use the superlative form.

ART

The Man with the Dog in the Gray Flannel Suit

Draw a cartoon illustrating your favorite misplaced modifier and, with your teacher's permission, post it in the hall where everybody can appreciate it.

GAME

Concentration

Do you remember those memory games—the ones with the cards turned face down? Here's a new twist on that old game. Write appropriate words on four groups of cards: nouns, adjectives, verbs, and adverbs. Then, lay all the cards out face down. Each player turns over two cards. If one card cannot sensibly modify the other, turn the cards back over. The player with the most matches wins.

Proofreading Application: Evaluation

Good writers are generally good proofreaders. Readers tend to admire writing that is error-free. Make sure that you correct all errors in grammar, usage, spelling, and punctuation in your writing. Your readers will have more confidence in your words if you have done your best to proofread carefully.

Whenever you make evaluations and comparisons, you use modifiers—adjectives and adverbs. If you don't use modifiers correctly, your readers may have trouble figuring out what they modify. Proofreading your modifiers will help you to communicate more effectively.

You can help your peers improve their writing by evaluating the content, organization, and usage in their writing. Make sure your evaluation uses modifiers correctly.

Proofreading Activity

In the following peer evaluation, find the errors in the use of modifiers and correct them. Use proofreading symbols such as those on page 935 of *Elements of Language* to make your corrections. If an item is already correct, write *C* above the item number.

Example **[1]** The writer's punctuation needs improvement ~~bad~~ badly.

[1] Overall, this opinion paper makes its point well. **[2]** Writing clearly and concisely, the thesis statement expresses the paper's content. **[3]** Another strong point is the description of works that were painted by Picasso in the opening paragraph. **[4]** The body of the paper is arranged logically, though a chronological order may have been more better. **[5]** Unfortunately, the emotional appeal in the conclusion was not as effective as in the introduction.

[6] Thinking back over the paper, the thing that impressed me most was my classmate's vocabulary. **[7]** This author seems to have a larger vocabulary than anyone in the class. **[8]** However, I had to read slow whenever I came across an unfamiliar word. **[9]** Some of the technical terms would have been least confusing if they had been defined. **[10]** Nevertheless, in only five pages, the author does give an effective answer to the question, "Which twentieth-century artist expresses life in the twentieth century better?"

Literary Model: Poetry

Sylvan historian, who canst thus express
A flowery tale more sweetly than our rhyme:

—from "Ode on a Grecian Urn"
by John Keats

Heard melodies are sweet, but those unheard
Are sweeter; therefore, ye soft pipes play on;

—from "Ode on a Grecian Urn"
by John Keats

With blackest moss the flower-pots
Were thickly crusted, one and all;

—from "Mariana"
by Alfred, Lord Tennyson

Three years she grew in sun and shower,
Then Nature said, "A lovelier flower
On earth was never sown;

—from "Three years she grew"
by William Wordsworth

Through what power,
Even for the least division of an hour,
Have I been so beguiled as to be blind
To my most grievous loss!—That thought's
return
Was the worst pang that sorrow ever bore,
Save one, one only, when I stood forlorn,
Knowing my heart's best treasure was no
more;

—from "Surprised by Joy"
by William Wordsworth

EXERCISE A Write each underlined modifier. Beside it, label it *positive*, *comparative*, or *superlative*.

EXERCISE B Write each underlined modifier. Beside it, write the word it modifies.

Literary Model (continued)

EXERCISE C Think about a memorable day of your life—a day that included good moments and not-so-good moments. Then, write a poem describing the day you have chosen. In your poem, be sure to use at least three comparative modifiers. (Try to use an interesting combination of positive, comparative, and superlative forms.) When you are finished, underline your modifiers that show comparison.

EXERCISE D Explain why it is sometimes more effective to use the comparative or superlative form of a modifier instead of the positive form (such as using *funniest* instead of *funny*).

Writing Application: Letter

You probably make at least one comparison a day—to say that basketball is a *more interesting* sport than soccer, to wonder why science seems so much *harder* than math, to announce that your favorite song is the *best* one on the air. Since comparing things seems to be an inherent part of human nature, you will naturally include comparisons when you write. Using comparisons that are clear and correctly formed will make any composition more polished.

UNCLEAR Tamika wrote her aunt more often than her cousin Tara.

CLEAR Tamika wrote her aunt more often **than she wrote her cousin Tara.**

CLEAR Tamika wrote her aunt more often **than her cousin Tara did.**

NONSTANDARD Arturo jumps higher than anyone on his team.

STANDARD Arturo jumps higher than anyone **else** on his team.

NONSTANDARD Your poem is more better than mine.

STANDARD Your poem is **better** than mine.

Writing Activity

Your best friend in fourth grade moved away at the end of that school year. The two of you have kept up a correspondence since then. The letter you received yesterday contained the announcement that your friend's family is moving back to your city. Your friend's parents know how much your city has grown and changed since they moved away, so they want feedback from you about which part of the city they should live in. In a personal letter to your friend, describe various parts of the real or imagined city you live in, using at least five comparative and five superlative forms of modifiers.

PREWRITING Arrange your ideas before you begin writing. You might create a big sketch of your city and jot down notes about the positive and negative aspects of living in each area. If you want to categorize information in a chart, you can use the names of the areas as column heads and use topics such as "Transportation," "Access to Stores," and "Noise Level."

WRITING As you write your draft, use the sketch or chart to help you make comparisons of the various parts of the city. Carefully choose comparative and superlative forms of modifiers so that each comparison will be clear to your friend.

REVISING Have a classmate play the role of your best friend and read the draft of your letter. Ask him or her to make sure all your comparisons are clear. Revise any comparisons that are confusing.

PUBLISHING Read your letter for errors in grammar, usage, spelling, and punctuation. Pay special attention to the spelling of comparative and superlative forms made by adding *–er* and *–est*. If you have included any of the eight troublesome modifiers discussed on pages 249–250 of your textbook, check that you have used them correctly. Then, neatly copy or print out your letter and add it to your portfolio.

Extending Your Writing

After completing your letter, work with a partner to create a brochure for an imaginary city. Your new city should have a combination of the best qualities that you and your partner described in your individual letters. Choose four or five of these qualities, then use text and illustrations to develop them.

NAME CLASS DATE

Choices: Exploring Real-World Usage

The following activities challenge you to find a connection between usage and the world around you. Do the activity below that suits your personality best, and then share your discoveries with your class.

ART

Road Signs

Create road signs cautioning against errors in usage. Begin by sketching road signs you see every day. You can find examples of many of these in a state-issued driver's manual or in a driver's education textbook. You may be surprised to learn that the shape of a road sign has a meaning. Incorporate these meanings into your designs. When the signs are completed, ask for permission to hang them around your school.

ANTHROPOLOGY

Other Voices

Language is closely bound to a person's cultural identity. Put yourself in an entirely new cultural situation; perhaps visit a new neighborhood, a business office, or a community center. Listen to how people talk in this setting. What do you hear that is unfamiliar to you? What aspects of the language are familiar? Share your findings with the class.

WRITING

Easy to Remember

Help your friends (or yourself) remember the solution to one or two troublesome usage problems. Write a rap, a riddle, or some other rhythmic lines that highlight the correct use of at least two of the items listed in this chapter. Then, teach your memory aid to the class.

WRITING

Get It Down

Every type of speech, even slang, has rules. You probably know more than a little slang. Write a glossary of ten current slang expressions. Define each word or expression, and include an example sentence for each one. Check with your teacher to be sure the items you have chosen are appropriate in the classroom. Then, share your glossary with the class.

GEOGRAPHY

Map It!

Many regions of the English-speaking world have their own special ways of talking. Dictionaries usually label these special usages *dialect* or *regionalism*. Most of these usages are informal, not incorrect. Research some regional and dialectal usages (*reckon, a-going, fixing to, y'uns, y'all*). Pay particular attention to expressions from your own region. Then, write each word or expression on a small piece of paper and pin it to a United States or world map, in the region where it is used. Post your map in the classroom.

MUSIC

"Froggie Went A-Courtin'"

Traditional songs like "Froggie Went A-Courtin'" contain examples of informal and nonstandard usage. In fact, nonstandard forms such as the prefix *a–* before a verbal can be quite useful to a songwriter because they add an extra beat. Write a humorous song in the traditional style. Include four or five informal or nonstandard items from the glossary chapter to help you maintain the rhythm or rhyme of your song. Then, play your song for the class. See if your classmates can identify the usage errors.

CREATIVE WRITING

Inside Out

You could say that English is really two languages—one for reading and writing and one for speaking. How well have you mastered both kinds of English? Find out. First, write a letter inviting friends to a casual dinner party. Use informal English in this letter. Next, use formal English to write a letter inviting friends and relatives to a very formal dinner party. Read both versions to the class.

Proofreading Application: Public Flyer

Good writers generally are good proofreaders. Readers tend to admire and trust writing that is error-free. Make sure that you correct all errors in grammar, usage, spelling, and punctuation in your writing. Readers will have more confidence in your words if you have done your best to proofread carefully.

Chances are that sooner or later you'll need to write a classified ad or a poster for your club or some other announcement. Your public statement is important to you. Proofread this type of document carefully so that usage errors do not threaten your success.

Proofreading Activity

Find and correct the errors in usage in the following flyer. Use proofreading symbols such as those on page 935 of *Elements of Language* to make your corrections.

Example Happyville schools need ~~you're~~ your help!

ATTENTION, Residents of Happyville!

Many schools in this district have no computers. The reason is because they are so expensive. Our classrooms were all suppose to have new computer systems by December of last year, but the money was spent on heating and cooling systems instead.

Students for Tomorrow, a group committed to our schools, must of already raised almost two thousand dollars. We've got a ways to go to reach our goal. We cannot succeed without you help us. Come to the

GIANT GARAGE SALE

on November 9 in the Happyville Middle School parking lot at 710 Oak Avenue.

Help Happyville students help theirselves. We need alot of donations! Give us that old toaster. Hand over them old tennis rackets. We need your white elephants. We won't turn down nothing. Your old televisions and radios are valuable to us; in fact, their our ticket to the technology of the future.

Drop off donations at Happyville Middle School, or call us at 555-6382! We pick up!

Literary Model: Description

They didn't know what to do. But like Cathy say, folks can't stand Granddaddy tall and silent and like a king. They can't neither. The smile the men smilin is pullin the mouth back and showin the teeth. Lookin like the wolf man, both of them. Then Granddaddy holds his hand out—this huge hand I used to sit in when I was a baby and he'd carry me through the house to my mother like I was a gift on a tray. Like he used to on the trains. They called the other men just waiters. But they spoke of Granddaddy separate and said, The Waiter. And said he had engines in his feet and motors in his hands and couldn't no train throw him off and couldn't nobody turn him around. They were big enough for motors, his hands were. He held that one hand out all still and it gettin to be not at all a hand but a person in itself.

—from "Blues Ain't No Mockin Bird" by Toni Cade Bambara

The following exercises will help you both to identify several common usage errors used in the preceding passage and to understand why the author chose to use them.

EXERCISE A

1. Identify the three double negatives in the passage, and write them on the line below.

____

2. Identify one use of *like* for which formal, standard usage would require *as*. Identify another use of *like* for which formal, standard usage would require *as if* or *as though*.

____

EXERCISE B

1. You may notice that not every negative expression in the passage is a double negative. Why do you think the narrator uses double negatives in the three places where they are used?

____

____

____

2. How would the tone of the passage be different if the narrator had consistently followed formal, standard usage rules regarding *like* and *as*?

____

____

Literary Model (continued)

EXERCISE C Write a paragraph in which a narrator describes someone he or she admires. In your description, try using informal or nonstandard expressions in a few places to help give the narrator a special voice and the paragraph a distinct tone and style.

EXERCISE D

1. What informal or nonstandard expressions did you use in your paragraph?

2. How did these informal or nonstandard expressions contribute to the voice of the narrator and affect the tone and style of the paragraph?

3. How did using informal or nonstandard expressions allow you to say things differently than if you had avoided using them?

Writing Application: Speech

When talking to friends, do you pay attention to whether you are using nonstandard or informal expressions? Of course, you don't. If you were talking to a potential employer during an interview, however, you would probably try to avoid all nonstandard and informal expressions in an effort to create a good impression.

INFORMAL/NONSTANDARD Didja make it to the concert last night? I would of, but I had to stay home with my sister. I heard it was totally cool.

FORMAL/STANDARD I would have preferred to work last summer as well, but I felt that it was more important to take the summer course work that will allow me to graduate a year in advance.

WRITING ACTIVITY

As student council representative for your class, you have been asked to present a four-minute speech to the school board on a topic of concern to students. In your speech, include at least five correct expressions covered in the standard usage guidelines in this chapter.

PREWRITING Determine the topic of your speech. Then, decide on a few questions you will ask your classmates about the topic. You will need to incorporate their opinions into your speech. Interview your classmates, and then categorize their responses in a chart. Then, create a rough outline using these responses, your own opinion, and other information needed to support the position you are expressing in the speech.

WRITING Use the outline to write a draft of your speech. Spend enough time on the introduction to make it grab your listeners' attention as you present your statement of opinion. Then, discuss each supporting point. Maintain your listeners' attention by making your speech focused and avoiding redundancy. Conclude your speech by restating your main point.

REVISING Ask a classmate to listen to your speech and to time it. Add or delete words to make the speech approximately four minutes long. Ask your classmate whether your position is clear, whether the speech is persuasive, and whether it contains any nonstandard or informal expressions that should be revised.

PUBLISHING Since this is a formal speech, check once more that it is free of usage problems and that you have used only formal, standard English. Use the glossary entries in this chapter to correct any common usage errors. With your teacher's permission, present your speech in front of the class.

EXTENDING YOUR WRITING

You could develop this writing exercise into a letter to the editor for your school, community, or school district newspaper.

Choices: Exploring Capitalization

The following activities challenge you to find a connection between capitalization and the world around you. Do the activity below that suits your personality best, and then share your discoveries with your class.

COMPUTER

Umbra BT

Computer software has wonderful and fantastic fonts, or alphabets. You probably have dozens of fonts on your computer. You can also find some very creative fonts in books of fonts. Pick out a few of the coolest ones, print them out, and label them. Not all fonts use lowercase letters. Which ones don't? Print them out, too. Then, post your printouts where everyone can see them.

VISUAL

Illuminated Manuscript

Go to the library, and find a copy of a page or two from the famous *Book of Kells*. Show the class how this beautiful manuscript uses capital letters. Point out differences between the way capital letters were used then and the way they are used now.

FOREIGN LANGUAGES

When in Rome

Research this question: Do all languages have capital letters? Which ones do not? Find an alphabet that does not use capital letters. Make a copy of the alphabet, and present your findings to the class.

RESEARCH

What's an Aitch, Anyway?

Answer this question. Then, explore the history of a capital letter, any letter. You'll be amazed! We owe the history of our letters to many cultures and peoples. Use a map as the basis of a poster illustrating the origins and development of just one capital letter.

REAL LIFE

Your Hometown

For each rule in this chapter, find a real-life example from your city or town. Then, write each rule, along with your hometown examples. Spice them up with some illustrations. Give your classmates copies for their notebooks.

DISCUSSION

Truth and Beauty

In the nineteenth century, English-language writers commonly capitalized a great many nouns. As time went on, this practice became more and more frowned upon. Generally, now only proper nouns are capitalized. However, nouns that refer to certain absolutes, such as Truth or Beauty, are still sometimes capitalized. Why do you suppose this change came about? To what political or cultural conditions would you attribute the change? Think about these questions. Then, lead your class in an exploration of these issues, using your opinions as a springboard for debate.

BUILDING BACKGROUND KNOWLEDGE

Under a Cabbage Leaf?

Research the words *uppercase* and *lowercase*. Where did these words originate? Prepare a report for the class about this interesting bit of historical background. Include illustrations, if possible.

REAL LIFE

In the Diplomatic Corps

Get a good secretarial dictionary, and check out the types of titles that people have in different parts of the world. How are these titles capitalized? Make a list of them, paying particular attention to interesting ones, as well as ones that you might actually have the need or opportunity to use in your life. Pass out copies of the list to your classmates for their notebooks.

Proofreading Application: Directions

Good writers are generally good proofreaders. Readers tend to admire and trust writing that is error-free. Make sure that you correct all errors in grammar, usage, spelling, and punctuation in your writing. Your readers will have more confidence in your words if you have done your best to proofread carefully.

Picture this: It is a hot summer day, and you have been walking eight blocks. You are now standing under a street sign that reads "Twelfth Street." In your hand is a crumpled page of handwritten directions. The directions say, "Turn left at the twelfth street sign." What do you do? Do you turn left now? Do you continue walking for another four blocks to the twelfth street sign? The instructions could be confusing.

If the writer had capitalized *Twelfth Street,* you would know what to do. Proper capitalization makes a writer's meaning clear. Be particularly careful to use capital letters correctly whenever you write directions.

Proofreading Activity

Find and correct the errors in capitalization in the following directions. Use proofreading symbols such as those on page 935 of *Elements of Language* to make your corrections.

Example if you follow these directions, you will find my house.

I know that you can get to the chinese restaurant on Connor drive, so start there. Go West on Connor Drive until you get to the American legion Hall. You should pass Parker lake on the way. That's the place where we held the car wash last Valentine's day. (Do you remember how we accidentally doused ms. Webb with soapy water?)

Cross the street. A methodist Church should be on your right. Every year, my family goes to the spring carnival there, by the way. Follow Twenty-First Street past Walnut elementary school.

I hope that all this walking hasn't worn a hole in those new High Flyer Sneakers that you got last week. You're almost there. Turn left at Jackson street. We're the third house on the right. It's the one with the ugliest plastic pink flamingos in north America standing right in the middle of the yard. How embarrassing they are!

NAME ______ CLASS ______ DATE ______

Literary Model: Using Capital Letters in Poetry

Fire and Ice

by Robert Frost

Some say the world will end in fire,
Some say in ice.
From what I've tasted of desire
I hold with those who favor fire.
But if it had to perish twice,
I think I know enough of hate
To say that for destruction ice
Is also great
And would suffice.

The Man from Washington

by James Welch

The end came easy for most of us.
Packed away in our crude beginnings
in some far corner of a flat world,
we didn't expect much more
than firewood and buffalo robes
to keep us warm. The man came down,
a slouching dwarf with rainwater eyes,
and spoke to us. He promised
that life would go on as usual,
that treaties would be signed, and everyone—
man, woman, and child—would be inoculated
against a world in which we had no part,
a world of money, promise, and disease.

EXERCISE A

1. What rule of capitalization does Frost follow but Welch break?

______

2. What do you think is Welch's method of deciding which words to capitalize?

______

EXERCISE B

1. How does Frost's use of capitalization affect your reading of his poem? For instance, do the capitals draw your attention to certain words, or do they create a particular sense of style?

______

______

______

______

NAME CLASS DATE

Literary Model (continued)

2. How does Welch's use of capitalization affect your reading of his poem?

EXERCISE C Write a poem using capitalization to emphasize certain words or images in a particular way or to create a distinct style. You may use capitalization as Frost does, as Welch does, or in some other way.

EXERCISE D How do you think your use of capitalization will affect a reader's understanding of your poem?

Writing Application: Giving Directions

Years ago, writers could capitalize words at their discretion and often capitalized any words—verbs, common nouns, pronouns—that they wanted to bring to readers' attention, as in this 1730 couplet written by Alexander Pope in praise of the mathematician Isaac Newton.

> Nature and Nature's Laws lay hid in Night:
> God said, Let NEWTON be: And all was Light!

Today, writers capitalize only proper nouns and adjectives (and sentences' first words, of course), but the goal is similar: The capital letter draws attention to the special nature of the words.

Writing Activity

Students at your school have planned a bike rally to raise funds for the community's food bank. Your job is to write the instructions for the bike rally. On the one hand, you need clear instructions so that all the riders make it to the rally's end. On the other hand, the directions should challenge the riders' navigational skills. In any case, capitalize all of the proper nouns and proper adjectives you use.

PREWRITING Most prewriting can be done at a desk or in the library. For this activity, you will need to take a map, paper, and pencil with you and drive, ride, or walk the route. A compass might help, too. Take notes on the names of streets, businesses, parks, housing divisions, and other places.

WRITING Organizing this writing assignment is easy: You must take riders from the route's beginning to its end. More challenging will be developing the right tone for this occasion and audience. Fund-raising for the food bank is a serious activity, but the bike rally itself should be fun for students. Your diction and word choice should contribute to the fun.

REVISING After you have completed your instructions, ask a friend to check their accuracy by riding the route. Ride along with the friend so that if the directions take him or her in the wrong direction, you can locate the problem and fix it. Also ask other students, as members of your audience, to comment on the tone of the instructions and make suggestions.

PUBLISHING Check the spelling, especially of place names, and punctuation of your instructions. Make sure that you have capitalized words such as *north* and *south* when they are part of a proper noun but not when they indicate which direction riders should travel. Distribute copies of your directions and copies of a map of the area. See which of your classmates can correctly mark the route on the map first.

Extending Your Writing

You may wish to develop this writing exercise further. While a bike rally is just for fun, knowing your way around your city is vital. You could develop and print a booklet to give to students who have recently moved into your school district, providing them with accurate directions to major city services, popular restaurants and stores, and school buildings such as stadiums.

Choices: Exploring End Marks, Abbreviations, Commas

The following activities challenge you to find a connection between end marks, abbreviations, and commas and the world around you. Do the activity below that suits your personality best, and then share your discoveries with your class.

PHOTOGRAPHY

Follow Your Nose

Commas are all around you. Take pictures or video footage of signs on streets, buses, subways—anywhere you find commas. Then, show your pictures to your classmates. Identify correct usage and errors. Finally, post your pictures (along with corrections!) in the classroom.

MUSIC

Wanted: Musicians

How are pauses indicated in musical notation? How are notes in a series separated or joined in musical notation? You know, but your classmates may not. Let them in on the secret. Explain what notations function as commas and as end marks in musical notation. Remember to create a handout for your classmates to keep in their notebooks.

DISCUSSION

WDEUA?

Why Does Everybody Use Acronyms? They seem to be everywhere. Sometimes a person can't even understand what is being said. "I need an ARF and a PO ASAP," said the VP. What's this lingo all about? Are we all really that pressed for time? Why is the number of acronyms increasing so fast? Research these questions, and write up a brief report. Then, share your findings with your classmates.

COMPUTER SCIENCE

Attention, Computer Experts!

Commas play important roles in computer programming. Do some research, and find out what commas do in one or more computer languages. For example, what happens when a comma is left out or put in the wrong place? Write up your findings, and share them with your classmates.

HISTORY

Calling Indiana Jones

Do a little linguistic archaeology. Find out when the practice of abbreviating began. Gather a few examples of early abbreviations, and share them with your class.

REAL LIFE

Be Prepared!

How should you address people from other countries? Find out the courtesy titles (words like *Mister*) that other cultures use. Learn how to write, abbreviate, and say them. You may want to consult language teachers at your school or foreign language speakers that you know. You could also consult a computerized dictionary that pronounces words. Complete the project by handing out a list of courtesy titles, their meanings, their language, and their abbreviations to your classmates.

SCIENCE

H_2O

How are abbreviations used in science? Roll out a copy of the periodic table, and expound on a few examples, pointing out their punctuation. In what other ways does science use and punctuate abbreviations?

ORIGINAL PROJECTS

Be Your Own Boss!

Make up your own project! Compose a collage of commas from headlines, ads, and magazines. Find strange uses of end marks, commas, and abbreviations. Then, discuss them with the class. Write and perform a dialogue between a comma and an end mark. Write a diary entry for a mark of punctuation. Dress up like a comma and be interviewed by the class. You name it; just do it! Be sure to get your teacher's approval for any project you decide to do.

Proofreading Application: Action Plan

Good writers are generally good proofreaders. Readers tend to admire and trust writing that is error-free. Make sure that you correct all errors in grammar, usage, spelling, and punctuation in your writing. Your readers will have more confidence in your words if you have done your best to proofread carefully.

Often during your school career, you will work on projects with other students. Team projects frequently require the exchange of written information. You will need to ask and answer questions, and you will need to relay lists of information. Sometimes, you will even need to give orders. For all of these messages, you will need to use end marks, abbreviations, and commas. Be a team player. Proofread carefully for correct punctuation so that your teammates can easily understand your messages.

Proofreading Activity

Find and correct the errors in end marks, abbreviations, and commas. Use proofreading symbols such as those on page 935 of *Elements of Language* to make your corrections.

Example 1. Could you scan Ms⊙ Mann's photographs into the computer, Jess. ?

OUR RESEARCH TEAM'S ACTION PLAN

Our Question

1. What is the current status of endangered species in Texas.

Step One

2. If possible Theresa you will interview Mr Vernon our science teacher.
3. Jess contact Sen Fisher at his office in Austin Texas.
4. Carlos, search the World Wide Web, for any relevant information
5. Since Lisa's mom works at the library Lisa will search current publications.

Step Two

6. Meet at 345 W Elm Ave on Saturday March 1 at 10:00 A.M. to pool data.

Step Three

7. Theresa will draw our maps, because she is the best artist.
8. Jess, didn't you agree to do the typing.
9. Carlos, will compile current statistics
10. Depending on need Lisa will do additional research; she will also proofread the first draft.

NAME ______________________ CLASS ______________ DATE ______________

Literary Model: Commas in a Description

Hunger stole upon me so slowly that at first I was not aware of what hunger really meant. Hunger had always been more or less at my elbow when I played, (1) but now I began to wake up at night and find hunger standing at my bedside, (2) staring at me gauntly. The hunger I had known before this had been no grim, (3) hostile stranger; it had been a normal hunger that had made me beg constantly for bread, (4) and when I ate a crust or two I was satisfied. But this new hunger baffled me, (5) scared me, (6) made me angry and insistent. Whenever I begged for food now, (7) my mother would pour me a cup of tea, (8) which would still the clamor in my stomach for a moment or two; but a little later I would feel hunger nudging my ribs, (9) twisting my empty guts until they ached. I would grow dizzy and my vision would dim. I became less active in my play, (10) and for the first time in my life I had to pause and think of what was happening to me.

—from *Black Boy* by Richard Wright

EXERCISE A For each numbered comma in the above passage, write one of the following letters on the lines provided to explain why the comma is used.

a. items in a series
b. two or more adjectives before a noun
c. independent clauses joined by a coordinating conjunction
d. nonessential clause or phrase
e. introductory adverb clause

1. __________ **4.** __________ **7.** __________ **9.** __________

2. __________ **5.** __________ **8.** __________ **10.** __________

3. __________ **6.** __________

EXERCISE B How does Wright's use of commas contribute to the sound and rhythm of the passage? (Hint: Try rewriting the passage so that it contains no commas, and read it aloud. What differences do you notice?)

____

____

____

Literary Model (continued)

EXERCISE C Write a short paragraph describing your first memory of a particular sensation, whether pleasant or unpleasant.

EXERCISE D

1. Now, rewrite two sentences of your paragraph, using commas to create a different rhythm or tone. For example, by using a comma and a coordinating conjunction, you could combine two sentences that express related thoughts, or you could use commas in a series to create an emphatic rhythm.

2. How did changing the way in which you used commas alter your sentences?

Writing Application: Script

Punctuation marks such as periods, exclamation points, question marks, and commas can easily be taken for granted. However, the function of a mark of punctuation is often crucial. For example, suppose you are Ted, and your swimming coach writes a note that says, "Ted, Ali and Diana have to swim forty laps." It makes a big difference whether the coach is addressing you or whether your name is one item in a series! Consider punctuation as a means of enhancing your writing, helping you separate your ideas, and showing the relationships between your ideas.

Writing Activity

You have been asked by a health promotion organization to write the script for a one-minute public service announcement. The announcement is intended for teenagers who listen to commercial radio stations. The script should be a dialogue between two teenagers who are providing information and persuading listeners to adopt a certain healthful behavior. Use end marks appropriately, and include at least one example of each of the following: a comma separating items in a series, a comma joining independent clauses, a comma setting off an introductory adverb clause, a comma setting off a noun of direct address, and a comma separating items in an address. Your end marks and commas will alert the actors to use appropriate intonation and pauses.

PREWRITING Choose the healthful behavior you will promote in your public service announcement script. Research the background information you need to write a script persuading teenagers to adopt the behavior. Take notes in an organized fashion as you read relevant literature or talk to experts. Also, take notes on the two characters you will create and the tone of their speech. Then, decide whether they will both promote the healthful behavior or whether one character will try to convince a reluctant second character to adopt the behavior.

WRITING Using your notes, write a draft of your script. Keeping your audience in mind as you write is very important. Try to be the writer and a representative of the audience at the same time. Don't overload the script with facts, but do include enough of them to support what you're trying to persuade your audience to do.

REVISING Ask two classmates to rehearse your script and then perform it for you and a third classmate. Encourage them to use the intonation and expression indicated by your use of punctuation. Listen critically to their delivery of the lines, and decide whether you need to make revisions to the content or punctuation. Ask the third classmate whether the script is persuasive and how it could be improved as a public service announcement.

PUBLISHING Proofread your script carefully, paying special attention to the use of commas and end marks. Check to be sure that you have included at least one example of each use of commas specified above. Then, perform your announcement for your class.

Extending Your Writing

You could develop this writing exercise into an actual script for a public service announcement to be aired at a community or commercial radio station. In addition, you might collect your classmates' scripts and present them to a staff member of the local branch of a relevant health organization with the suggestion that they could be used as the basis for future public service announcements.

Choices: Exploring Semicolons and Colons

The following activities challenge you to find a connection between punctuation marks and the world around you. Do the activity below that suits your personality best, and then share your discoveries with your class.

PUBLISHING

On Safari

Go on a scavenger hunt for colons and semicolons. Look in newspapers, magazines, billboards, and other published sources to find places where a colon or a semicolon might be hiding. Then, photograph or cut them out and paste them to poster board. Be sure to note whether each colon or semicolon has been used correctly or incorrectly.

MATH AND SCIENCE

10:1

Colons are a rather all-purpose mark of punctuation, aren't they? They can identify a Bible verse just as easily as they can draw your attention to a grocery list. Besides the uses listed in your textbook, what other uses of colons can you find? Check out a scientific book, or page through a math text for starters. When you've found a few examples, fill the class in on your discoveries.

POSTER

What's Your Title?

Once you start to look around, you will notice that many titles of books and movies contain a colon. On a piece of poster board, write down at least five movie titles and at least five book titles that contain a colon. You can decorate your poster however you want, but make sure your titles are bold and easy to read. With your teacher's permission, post your list in the classroom.

ANALYSIS

Alike and Different

Why do we bother to have both commas and semicolons? What's the difference? Think about it. Make a chart that has two columns: one labeled "Similarities" and the other labeled "Differences." Then, brainstorm ways in which commas and semicolons are alike and ways in which they are different. When you're finished, copy your chart onto poster board and show your findings to the class.

DEBATE

The One and Only

Get together with two classmates, and stage an argument among a period, a semicolon, and a comma. Each one thinks that it is the best way of dividing independent clauses and that the other marks should get lost. Naturally, you'll want to stay in character. Mr. or Ms. Semicolon wouldn't use commas and conjunctions to divide independent clauses! Videotape or perform your debate for the class.

COMPUTER SCIENCE

Technical Language

How are colons and semicolons used in computer science? How do computer languages use these marks of punctuation? Choose a computer language, and give several examples of code that include semicolons and colons. Explain to the class the functions of colons and semicolons in the sample code that you chose.

INVENTION

Make Your Mark

It's a new century! Design a new mark of punctuation for our changing times. You'll need a shape, a name, and a purpose for your mark. Begin by considering what new situations, such as e-mail, may need such a mark.

Proofreading Application: Minutes of a Meeting

Good writers are generally good proofreaders. Readers tend to admire and trust writing that is error-free. Make sure that you correct all errors in grammar, usage, spelling, and punctuation in your writing. Your readers will have more confidence in your words if you have done your best to proofread carefully.

Proofreading Activity

In the following minutes of a meeting, find and correct the errors in the use of semicolons and colons. Use proofreading symbols such as those on page 935 of *Elements of Language* to make your corrections.

Example The minutes of a meeting are ; notes on everything that happened.

Karen Wood opened the meeting on Wednesday, November 11. Then, Bill Nichols took roll. The minutes were read by Thomas Birch no corrections were made. Old business included: setting the date for the carnival, purchasing a plaque for Mr. Polanski, and appointing a new treasurer.

Lisa Galen proposed the following dates for the carnival, Saturday, April 10, Saturday, April 24, and Saturday, May 1. Neil Voight moved to make April 24 the date of the carnival, Kenji Chase seconded the motion, which carried unanimously.

Susan Radding moved that the club engrave the Biblical passage John 1 1 on Mr. Polanski's plaque. Some objections were voiced by: Thomas Birch, Otis Frank, and Sally Dawson; however, alternative passages could not be agreed upon, and the motion was seconded by Lee Chan and carried with one dissenting vote.

Karen Wood appointed Lee Chan treasurer, however, Lee Chan declined, and the chair appointed Neil Voight, who accepted. Sarah Mendoza moved that the meeting be adjourned so that she could call the trophy shop to order the plaque; the motion was seconded by Otis Frank. The meeting was adjourned at 4 18 P.M.; the next meeting is scheduled for Wednesday, November 18.

Literary Model: Semicolons in a Novel

Such a bustle ensued that you might have thought a goose the rarest of all birds; a feathered phenomenon, to which a black swan was a matter of course; and in truth it was something very like it in that house. Mrs. Cratchit made the gravy (ready beforehand in a little saucepan) hissing hot; Master Peter mashed the potatoes with incredible vigor; Miss Belinda sweetened up the applesauce; Martha dusted the hot plates; Bob took Tiny Tim beside him in a tiny corner at the table; the two young Cratchits set chairs for everybody, not forgetting themselves, and mounting guard upon their posts, crammed spoons into their mouths, lest they should shriek for goose before their turn came to be helped.

—from *A Christmas Carol* by Charles Dickens

EXERCISE A

1. How many sentences are in the passage? ________________

2. Which semicolon breaks a rule of punctuation by joining an independent clause with a sentence fragment?

____

EXERCISE B

1. Why do you think Dickens used numerous semicolons in this passage instead of periods?

____

____

____

2. If Dickens had used periods in place of most of the semicolons, would the paragraph read differently? How? Do the semicolons reinforce the sense of "bustle"? Explain your answers.

____

____

____

____

____

____

Literary Model (continued)

EXERCISE C Write a paragraph describing an occasion when you shared a meal with friends or family. Use semicolons to join some or all of the clauses.

EXERCISE D

1. How did you decide where to use semicolons and where to use periods in your paragraph?

2. Read your paragraph aloud. How do the semicolons affect how the paragraph sounds? Do you read over them more quickly or more slowly than you read over periods?

Writing Application: Business Letter

On a city street, flashing lights and neon signs draw people's attention to certain details. Even when the street is busy, its yellow caution lights stand out and warn distracted drivers of hazards. Colons can function in a similar way, directing readers' attention to important sentence elements that otherwise may go unnoticed. When used effectively, colons allow writers to make sentences more interesting and emphatic.

LESS EMPHATIC Precision is important in engineering.

MORE EMPHATIC In engineering, one concern matters greatly**:** precision.

By isolating the word *precision* with a colon, the writer draws attention to it.

Writing Activity

Pick up a copy of your favorite magazine. No matter how good it is, it could be better, and you are just the person to say how. Write a letter to the editors, complimenting them on what you like about the magazine and suggesting specific problems that they might address to improve it. Use colons to draw the busy editors' attention to the important points in your letter.

PREWRITING Thumb through the magazine, jotting down notes about what you especially like. Then, think about what bothers you about the magazine: too many ads? not enough photographs? Perhaps you are looking for more advice from the writers. Dig deeply for what you would like to see changed. Finally, consult the magazine's inside cover for the names and address of the editors.

WRITING Consider how you will organize your material, remembering that business letters are brief and to the point. Should you first address what you like about the magazine, or should you present the problems first? How will editors react to your chosen pattern of organization?

REVISING Ask a friend or family member to read your letter and let you know if he or she has trouble understanding its organization or if your tone needs improvement. Make sure you have used the correct format for a business letter.

PUBLISHING No truer test of writing exists than getting the chance to have your intended audience read what you wrote. Check your letter for spelling and punctuation. Watch especially for correctly placed colons. Finally, print out and mail your letter.

Extending Your Writing

You might make your letter a starting point for an essay in which you analyze the effectiveness of one printed publication. Consider addressing both design and content issues. Be sure to share your essay with the editors of whatever publication you analyze.

Choices: Exploring Italics and Quotation Marks

The following activities challenge you to find a connection between italics and quotation marks and the world around you. Do the activity below that suits your personality best, and then share your discoveries with your class.

BUILDING BACKGROUND KNOWLEDGE

Top Forty

Take a poll of your class. What are your classmates' forty favorite novels? Publish your list, with titles in italics, of course. Then, with your teacher's permission, post the results of your poll where everyone can read them.

TEACHING

Be a Teacher

Teach some elementary-school students how to use quotation marks. Let the young students dictate a dialogue to you. Then, show them where the quotation marks go. Third-, fourth-, and fifth-graders have loads of stories to tell.

RESEARCH

Chirp, Shout, or Mumble

Since you'll be writing some dialogue for Chapter 13, you'll need a few synonyms for *said*. Do yourself and your class a favor; make a list of these synonyms. You may want to divide the list into categories, such as volume or emotion. Then, pass out copies of your list.

WRITING

Book of Life

Do you have a favorite quotation that sums up your philosophy of life? If you do, write it down. If you don't, find one. Then, ask your classmates to do the same. Gather all the quotations, and either write or type them one quote to a page. Be sure to use proper quotation marks and end marks. Print them out in different fonts. You might also want to include a picture of each classmate on the page with his or her quote. Design a cover for your book, and bind it. With your teacher's permission, display it in the classroom.

READING AND WRITING

In the Screenwriters Guild

Playwrights and scriptwriters don't use quotation marks. How do they distinguish spoken language? Find out. Then, script a page of dialogue to serve as a model for your classmates. Share your speculations on why scripts do not use quotation marks. Also, point out how colons are used in scripts. Are there any other scriptwriting punctuation conventions you can explain to your class?

POPULAR CULTURE

We're "Open" All Night

Have you ever noticed that some people use quotation marks for emphasis rather than to indicate that someone is being quoted? Are there any signs, public notices, or even local menus you've seen that say things like *We sell "jumbo hot dogs" and "hamburgers"* or *We're "open" all day Sunday*? Have you ever noticed people using their index and middle fingers to represent quotation marks as they talk when they want to indicate that a term is meant ironically? What do you make of these and other real-world uses of quotation marks? Document some unusual uses, and share your findings with your class.

ORIGINAL PROJECTS

Break the Mold

Want to create a project of your own? Open your eyes and look around. You could write a report, give a presentation, or make a collage about what you see. Write an essay telling how you would use quotation marks and italics if you could make the rules. Better yet, show the class how you would do it. Design a T-shirt using quotation marks and italics. Come up with some other project that only you could design. Be sure to get your teacher's approval before proceeding with your plan.

Proofreading Application: Written Interview

Good writers generally are good proofreaders. Readers tend to admire and trust writing that is error-free. Make sure that you correct all errors in grammar, usage, spelling, and punctuation in your writing. Your readers will have more confidence in your words if you have done your best to proofread carefully.

When you use a person's exact words, proofread your use of quotation marks carefully. If you don't, your readers may have difficulty figuring out who said what. Using italics or underlining correctly to distinguish titles of works such as books, plays, and periodicals is also important to avoid confusing your reader.

Proofreading Activity

Find and correct the errors in the use of quotation marks and italics in the following written interview. Use proofreading symbols such as those on page 935 of *Elements of Language* to make your corrections.

Example I wrote this interview for the school newspaper "Lion's Roar"

"I never liked English very much, Ms. Gina Paulson, our new ninth-grade English teacher claims, "until I was in ninth grade." "That year I read the novel Summer of the Swans. Until then, I thought that stories had to be about larger-than-life events.

A bit surprised, I nod, remembering dramatic plays like Shakespeare's *Julius Caesar*. This interview is not going as I expected.

But the swan story was about an ordinary girl in an ordinary situation." Ms. Paulson continues. "I started to write my own stories about ordinary things, and English became more interesting. "I actually published one in *Plains Review*.

"What was the name of your story"? I ask.

"Paper Airplanes, she says. It's about using your imagination to solve problems.

"I see," I answer. Do you ever find that using your imagination to write a story leads you to the solution of a problem of your own?"

The talkative Ms. Paulson has nothing to say. She just smiles.

Literary Model: Dialogue in Poetry

from "The Lesson of the Moth"
by Don Marquis

why do you fellows
pull this stunt i asked him
because it is the conventional thing for moths or why
. . . .
have you no sense
plenty of it he answered
but at times we get tired
of using it
we get bored with the routine
and crave beauty
and excitement
fire is beautiful
and we know that if we get
too close it will kill us
but what does that matter

EXERCISE A Rewrite the dialogue above as if it were a printed dialogue rather than a poem. Add end marks, commas, quotation marks, and capital letters where they are needed. Begin a new paragraph every time the speaker changes.

EXERCISE B Don Marquis explained this poem's lack of capitalization and punctuation by claiming that the poem was written by a cockroach named archy. In addition to reflecting archy's typing problems, how does the lack of punctuation and capitalization help characterize archy?

Literary Model (continued)

EXERCISE C Write a poem that contains dialogue. First, brainstorm possible conversations that you would like to express in a poem. Then, decide whether the scenario you like best calls for standard use of quotation marks and other punctuation.

EXERCISE D

1. Did you use standard punctuation in your poem? Why or why not?

2. If you did use standard punctuation, how would your poem be different if you had written it without standard punctuation? Would the style or meaning be different? Would readers experience the poem the same way? Explain.

3. If you did not use standard punctuation, how does the lack of standard punctuation contribute to the style or meaning of the poem? Do you think readers will experience your poem the same way as they would if you had used standard punctuation? Explain.

Writing Application: Dialogue

No matter how formal the writing context, writers add interest when they let readers "hear" what someone has said. An individual's choice of words tells us much that we may not learn from indirect quotations.

INDIRECT Miguel says that he is planning to audition for the lead role in the play.

DIRECT Miguel mused, "I'm not sure . . . maybe I should try out for the lead."

DIRECT Miguel announced, "Of course, I'm auditioning—I was born to play that role!"

The indirect quotation tells us only that Miguel plans to audition, but his exact words reveal his attitude and level of confidence, too.

Writing Activity

Often, teens need to ask adults' permission before participating in various group events—going to an amusement park or taking a camping trip, for example. Think of an upcoming event that you will need to discuss with either a parent or guardian. Write a conversation, using dialogue, in which you and the adult decide on guidelines for your participation in the event.

PREWRITING List the details about the event as you will present them to the parent or guardian. Then, imagine questions that an adult might raise and the answers you will give. Anticipate whether the adult will be in favor of your participation; if not, brainstorm ways to persuade the adult.

WRITING As you write the dialogue, decide what words you will use to present your case. Imagine also the words the adult might use in reply. Try to capture each speaker's attitude toward the event.

REVISING Writers can choose from many words as they introduce quotations. Avoid overusing the verb *say*; instead, vary the verb you use to identify someone's words. Sometimes we simply say words; at other times, we insist, plead, cajole, argue, or suggest!

PUBLISHING Check your dialogue for errors in usage, punctuation, and spelling. Make sure that you have placed end marks and commas correctly in relation to closing quotation marks and that you have begun a new paragraph each time the speaker changes. With a friend, read your dialogue in front of the class.

Extending Your Writing

You may wish to develop this writing exercise further. For instance, you could write an essay teaching teens how to better communicate with the important adults in their lives, inserting short dialogues to demonstrate how to keep communication lines open (and how they sometimes get shut down); or you could expand the dialogue you have written into a one-act play that focuses on relationships between teens and adults.

Choices: Exploring Apostrophes

The following activities challenge you to find a connection between apostrophes and the world around you. Do the activity below that suits your personality best, and then share your discoveries with your class.

ART

Bigger Is Better

First, outline a giant apostrophe on poster board. Then, inside the apostrophe, write as many common and uncommon contractions and plurals (those that are formed with apostrophes) as you can. Naturally, you'll want to include a few that refer to your class, the students in it, and your projects. Why not make the apostrophes red or a contrasting color?

GAMES

Brothers But Not Sisters

Compile a list of irregular plural nouns, such as *oxen*. Make it a long list. Then, have some fun! With your teacher's permission, divide the class into two teams. Then, say each singular noun aloud. The first team to give the correct irregular plural and its possessive form wins! Oh, why is the title of this project "Brothers But Not Sisters"? The irregular plural for *brother* is *brethren*, but *sisters* doesn't have an irregular plural. Now, invent your own list of irregulars.

WRITING

The Challenge

Can you write a sentence that contains an apostrophe in every single word? Can anyone? You'll never know until you try. Try it! Better yet, have a contest to see who can write the longest sentence in which every word uses an apostrophe. Yes, of course, questions are allowed.

DISCUSSION

The *I's* Have It

Are there any words or types of words, such as parts of speech, that cannot be used with an apostrophe, either in a plural or a contraction? Hmmmm. With your teacher's permission, lead a class discussion. During the discussion, write example sentences on the chalkboard showing different parts of speech and the ways they take apostrophes.

BUILDING BACKGROUND KNOWLEDGE

Sioux Relatives

Compile a list of nouns that do not change forms when they are used as plurals. Then, write two sentences—one using the singular possessive and the second using the plural possessive of each noun. Alphabetize your list and print it out double spaced so that there's room for new entries. Give your classmates copies for their notebooks.

WRITING

Tongue Twister

Write a tongue twister using the words *whose* and *who's*. Increase the difficulty of your twister by using words that rhyme or almost rhyme with *who* and by using words that start with the same sound as *who*. Who knows? Your tongue twister may enter popular culture and outlive you by a century or two!

DISCUSSION

Listen Closely

Come up with a list of names that end with *s*. A book of baby names would be a good place to start. Then, for each name, decide whether the possessive of that name should be followed by just an apostrophe or by an apostrophe and an *s*. Explain your reasoning when you submit your list, item by item, for the class's approval. Expect some disagreement!

DRAMA

Center Stage

Take one particularly fine example of writing that includes dialogue containing a lot of contractions. Then, rewrite it without using contractions. Perform both versions of the dialogue (ask one or more friends to help out if more than one character is speaking). Finally, lead a discussion of what is gained or lost by changing all the contractions.

NAME CLASS DATE

Proofreading Application: Newspaper Article

Good writers are generally good proofreaders. Readers tend to admire and trust writing that is error-free. Make sure that you correct all errors in grammar, usage, spelling, and punctuation in your writing. Your readers will have more confidence in your words if you have done your best to proofread carefully.

Proper use of apostrophes is especially important in informative writing, in which accurate and clear information is essential. However, when a writer uses apostrophes improperly, the meaning of information can become fuzzy and readers can become confused and frustrated. Provide accurate and clear information for your readers by proofreading your writing carefully to avoid errors in the use of apostrophes.

Proofreading Activity

In the following newspaper article, find the errors in the use of apostrophes and replace the incorrect words. Use proofreading symbols such as those on page 935 of *Elements of Language* to make your corrections. An item may contain more than one error.

Example The student's now have an Exploratorium!

Last Friday was opening day for the new Exploratorium for Winn Elementarys students. At two o clock, Principal Brenda Jaffe cut the big red ribbon, and dozens of third-graders streamed into the show. "The futures yours'," Ms. Jaffe told her students.

Twenty-four colorful displays lined the walls of a portable class room devoted to the project. Jason Perez's and Celia Emerson's giant soap-bubble machine drew *ooh*s and *ah*s from the pint-sized scientists. Jim Washington wasn't surprised to see the eager visitors flock to his' rainbow machine, which dazzled onlookers. Kyle Smith and Lisa White Deer's smiles drew almost as big a crowd as their magnet displays, which appeared to fascinate their fan's. Another group of student's clustered around the mices cage in which an energetic pair of rodents powered a tiny windmill.

Planning, funding, and completing the exhibits construction took an entire semester of the Young Scientists Saturday afternoons. Take your bow, Young Scientists'; all that work was worth it!

NAME ______ CLASS ______ DATE ______

Literary Model: Poetic Description

Mercutio.

O, then I see Queen Mab hath been with
you.
She is the fairies' midwife, and she comes
In shape no bigger than an agate stone
On the forefinger of an alderman,
Drawn with a team of little atomies
Over men's noses as they lie asleep;
Her wagon spokes made of long spinners'
legs,
The cover, of the wings of grasshoppers;
Her traces, of the smallest spider web;
Her collars, of the moonshine's wat'ry
beams;
Her whip, of cricket's bone; the lash, of
film;
Her wagoner, a small gray-coated gnat,
Not half so big as a round little worm
Pricked from the lazy finger of a maid;
Her chariot is an empty hazelnut,
Made by the joiner squirrel or old grub,
Time out o' mind the fairies' coachmakers.
And in this state she gallops night by night
Through lovers' brains, and then they
dream of love;
On courtiers' knees, that dream on curt-
sies straight;
O'er lawyers' fingers, who straight dream
on fees;
O'er ladies' lips, who straight on kisses
dream. . . .
Sometime she gallops o'er a courtier's nose,
And then dreams he of smelling out a
suit;
And sometimes comes she with a tithe
pig's tail
Tickling a parson's nose as [he] lies
asleep,
Then dreams he of another benefice.

—from *Romeo and Juliet* by William Shakespeare
Act I, Scene 4

EXERCISE A

1. How many of the underlined words in the passage above are singular possessives? ______
2. How many are plural possessives? ______
3. How many are contractions? ______
4. Why do you think Shakespeare uses contractions instead of spelling out the words? ______

______

______

______

______

______

Literary Model (continued)

EXERCISE B On the lines below, write a short description of an imaginary creature or person. In your description, give the being a name, explain what it looks like, and describe what fantastic powers it has. You may choose to write your description in verse, as Shakespeare did.

EXERCISE C

1. In what words did you use an apostrophe to show possession?

2. In what words did you use an apostrophe to form a contraction?

3. How do the contractions you used contribute to the tone of your description? If you wrote your description in verse, how do the contractions affect the meter, or poetic rhythm, of your description?

Writing Application: Newspaper Article

When you were in a preschool or kindergarten class, some type of label probably served to connect you and your name with your lunchbox, book bag, and other possessions. In a way, the apostrophe serves a similar purpose: In writing, it connects an object with its owner.

WRITING ACTIVITY

For the sports section of a high school or local newspaper, write an article describing an athletic event. As you mention details such as whose free throw won the game and whose defense techniques were masterful, use at least three singular possessive nouns, two plural possessive nouns, and two indefinite pronouns in the possessive case.

PREWRITING Either attend an athletic event, spend several minutes recalling one you attended in the past, or make up an athletic event in your head—complete with many details. Jot down phrases and complete sentences that answer the six questions crucial to any newspaper article: *Who? What? When? Where? Why?* and *How?* In addition, since all athletic events involve some kind of action, and actions are expressed by verbs, brainstorm a list of verbs you can use that are particularly descriptive and lively. If necessary, read articles from the sports section of a few newspapers to get ideas.

WRITING Craft an opening sentence that makes your reader want to read the entire article. Use the verbs you brainstormed—or others that may pop into your head once you get in the rhythm of writing about the athletic event. If you're still not satisfied with your choice of verbs, consult a thesaurus. Remember, however, to double-check a dictionary to be sure that a word suggested by the thesaurus is appropriate for your context.

REVISING Read your draft aloud. Listen for weak words and clichés, and replace any you find with exciting words and phrases that you use in a novel way. If your draft contains few sensory details—details observed through sight, hearing, taste, touch, or smell—consider adding some. Make the reader feel as if he or she were actually at the athletic event. Pay special attention to your use of apostrophes. Make sure you haven't confused possessive pronouns with contractions and that you used at least three singular possessive nouns, two plural possessive nouns, and two indefinite pronouns in the possessive case.

PUBLISHING Proofread your newspaper article line by line to correct errors in spelling, grammar, and punctuation. Try designing your composition to look like an actual newspaper article. Choose a name for your publication, and write a headline for your sports story. If your class has a Web site, ask your teacher for permission to post your story online.

EXTENDING YOUR WRITING

Perhaps you could transfer what you have learned to a group of middle school students enrolled in an after-school program. You could read them your article and suggest tips for writing a successful newspaper article about an athletic event. Then, play the role of teacher as you assign them to write their own article and "coach" them during the writing process.

Choices: Exploring Punctuation

The following activities challenge you to find a connection between punctuation and the world around you. Do the activity below that suits your personality best, and then share your discoveries with your class.

HISTORY

1492

Do you know what happened in 1492? Of course you do. It's one of the dates that every American should know. Create a list of what you consider to be important dates in world and American history—ten or twenty should be enough. Then, write sentences for each event and put the appropriate date in parentheses. Cut out your sentences, and paste them in order on a time line.

MATHEMATICS

$a(b+c)$

How are parentheses used in mathematics, especially in algebra? Find some good examples and explain them to the class. Make connections between your examples and terms that the class already knows, such as subject, predicate, complement, and clause. You may wish to transform equations into words.

COMPUTER

:) or :(

Do you surf the Net? Internet users have some interesting uses for punctuation. Find out as much as you can about the language of the Internet. For example, find a list of *emoticons* and discover what is *netiquette*? Then, tell (and show) your classmates how punctuation marks are used on the Internet.

ETYMOLOGY

Dashing and Daring

What exactly does the word *dash* mean? How many definitions does it have? What are the origins of the word? Find out. Then, write sentences using each definition. Make a poster using your etymology, definitions, and sentences. With your teacher's permission, hang it in plain view of your classmates.

WRITING

Acronym Alert

Isn't it frustrating when you suddenly come across a group of capital letters in something you're reading, but the writer doesn't tell you what they mean? If your class hasn't already compiled a list of acronyms, such as FBI and IRS, do so now. Be sure to include the full name of each agency or organization. A telephone book is a good source for many acronyms. Write sentences using each acronym. In parentheses, spell out the full name of each acronym. Then, make a poster displaying your list and sentences. With your teacher's permission, hang your poster in the classroom.

COMPUTER

Test Pilot

Many word-processing programs will hyphenate words automatically. However, a computer's hyphenation is seldom as good as yours. Turn on and off automatic hyphenation in a word-processing program and do an experiment. Turn on hyphenation, and set very wide margins. Type in a paragraph or two, and print the paragraphs out. Check the computer's hyphenation against a dictionary's. Report your findings to the class, advising them either to turn on or to turn off automatic hyphenation.

ORIGINAL PROJECTS

Custom-made

Create a custom-made project that suits your interests. If you like reading, find a passage that uses every mark of punctuation. If you like writing, write that passage. If you like science, investigate how science uses punctuation marks. Collect examples of dashes. Figure out a way to use a computer program to check that every open parenthesis has a closed parenthesis. Whatever project you choose, be sure to get your teacher's approval before you begin.

Proofreading Application: Advertising Flier

Good writers are generally good proofreaders. Readers tend to admire and trust writing that is error-free. Make sure that you correct all errors in grammar, usage, spelling, and punctuation in your writing. Your readers will have more confidence in your words if you have done your best to proofread carefully.

Fliers are one of the most inexpensive ways of advertising. In a single page, a flier can give the public a great deal of information about an event or service. When you write a flier, pay particular attention to proofreading for correct use of the punctuation marks you have studied in this chapter. Give special attention to parentheses and brackets. If you leave out one half of a pair, many of your readers will be lost because they won't understand you.

Proofreading Activity

In the following flier, find the errors in the use of hyphens, dashes, parentheses, brackets, and ellipsis points and correct them. Use proofreading symbols such as those on page 935 of *Elements of Language* to make your corrections.

Example Joel's business—he takes care of pets—is doing quite well.

Joel's Pet Sitting Service

546 Fifty seventh Street

Your pets—dogs, cats, birds, ponies, iguanas, and tropical fish are our specialty!

Our business is pet sitting, but we don't just sit!

We offer feeding, walking, washing elephants require an extra charge), and tender loving care.

Even exotic pets (we once cared for a boa constrictor (her name was Nancy) are no problem for us! Your beloved pet won't suffer a moment's discomfort or loneliness when we are on the job!

Call 555 5442 555 4455 after 4:00 P.M.

Three-quarters of our customers use our services more than once!

The following is a testimony from Mrs. Rhonda Peal, one of our loyal customers:

"My three dogs and two cats love Joel. He has been my pet sitter many times . . . and I have found him to be dependable and kind."

NAME ______ CLASS ______ DATE ______

Literary Model: Dashes in a Story

The stranger looked at me again—still cocking his eye, as if he were expressly taking aim at me with his invisible gun—and said, 'He's a likely young parcel of bones that. What is it you call him?'

'Pip,' said Joe.

'Christened Pip?'

'No, not christened Pip.'

'Surname Pip?'

'No,' said Joe, 'it's a kind of family name what he gave himself when an infant, and is called by.'

'Son of yours?'

'Well,' said Joe, meditatively—not, of course, that it could be in anywise necessary to consider about it, but because it was the way at the Jolly Bargemen to seem to consider deeply about everything that was discussed over pipes; 'well—no. No, he ain't.'

'Nevvy?' said the strange man.

'Well,' said Joe, with the same appearance of profound cogitation, 'he is not—no, not to deceive you, he is *not*—my nevvy.'

'What the Blue Blazes is he?' asked the stranger. Which appeared to me to be an inquiry of unnecessary strength.

—from *Great Expectations* by Charles Dickens

EXERCISE A In the excerpt above, circle four places where Dickens uses dashes to indicate abrupt breaks in thought or to introduce an explanation. Hint: Two dashes used to set off one element count as a single use.

EXERCISE B

1. What do the dashes in Joe's speech indicate about how he talks and feels in this situation?

______

______

______

______

2. What do the dashes in the narration indicate about the way the narrator (Pip) talks and how he feels describing this scene?

______

______

______

______

Literary Model (continued)

EXERCISE C Think about a time when a friend or family member introduced you to someone you didn't know—for example, on the first day of school or at a family gathering. If the meeting was unexpected or the person you were being introduced to kept asking questions, the situation may have been a little uncomfortable. Write a short dialogue portraying such a scene, whether it's an actual event or one that you imagine. Use dashes to indicate abrupt breaks in thought or to mean *namely* or *that is.*

EXERCISE D

1. How did you use dashes to indicate how you felt while you were being introduced?

2. How did you use dashes to indicate how the person introducing you and the stranger you were being introduced to felt?

Writing Application: Reports

Each element of punctuation has specific functions that help you make your writing as clear as possible. Some elements help your reader understand the relationships among the words and ideas you are trying to get across. For example, when you write "My great-aunt Roberta (she's 78 years young) is an amazing storyteller," your reader realizes that the information in parentheses is less important than your great-aunt's storytelling abilities. Other elements of punctuation are like road signs in that they provide specific information. Ellipsis points, for instance, can indicate that something has been omitted from quoted materials.

WRITING ACTIVITY

Mentally walk yourself through a typical day. Pause whenever you visualize yourself using an ordinary object. At the end of your mental stroll, choose one of the ordinary objects you imagined and use it as the topic of a short report. In no more than three paragraphs, describe how the object came into existence and, if applicable, how its function has changed over time. Use at least three of the five elements of punctuation (hyphens, dashes, parentheses, brackets, and ellipsis points) discussed in this chapter.

PREWRITING You'll need to locate and read information about the object in reference sources. To read with a purpose, apply the following techniques: Don't start off by reading from the first page of the reference source. Look for key words in the index, study the table of contents, and skim text to check headings, charts, and illustrations. When you find information on your topic, slow down and read every word. Take notes on main ideas and specific details. Don't copy every word into your notes; use your own words instead. However, you may want to use one or two direct quotations in your report. Be sure you keep track of the sources that contain relevant information.

WRITING Use your notes to write a draft. Spend extra time on your opening sentence; a well-crafted opening sentence will entice your reader to continue. Clearly connect and arrange the ideas in chronological order. In addition, use transitional words and phrases to show how the ideas are connected.

REVISING Set your draft aside for a while before you begin final revisions. When you read the report again, ask yourself whether you could improve it by including quoted material from one of your sources. If so, use ellipsis points correctly if you decide to omit parts of the material. Be sure that you have used at least three of the five elements of punctuation mentioned above.

PUBLISHING Proofread your report for errors in spelling, grammar, and punctuation. In particular, ask yourself whether every sentence is a complete sentence, whether the tense and form of each verb are correct, and whether the report is free of errors in subject-verb and pronoun-antecedent agreement. Double-check your use of hyphens, dashes, parentheses, brackets, and ellipsis points for correctness and clarity. With your teacher's permission, post your report on the class bulletin board or Web page.

EXTENDING YOUR WRITING

Collect your classmates' reports. Create an anthology titled *Extraordinary Histories of Ordinary Objects*. Exchange anthologies with other classes or donate yours to the school library.

Choices: Exploring Spelling

The following activities challenge you to find a connection between spelling and the world around you. Do the activity below that suits your personality best, and then share your discoveries with your class.

LINGUISTICS

Pore, Poor, and *Pour*

The homonyms that you see in your textbook are not the only ones in English. What are some of the other homonyms that can often be confused? Make an alphabetized list of at least ten of these word pairs and their definitions. Be sure to make copies to hand out to your classmates.

GEOGRAPHY

From Arabia to India to England

Show the class how American English has borrowed words from every continent in the world. Copy or sketch a good-sized world map. Then, trace the path of ten words as they entered the English language.

RESEARCH

Swahili or Cherokee?

When English-language speakers hear a good word, they remember it. Oh, sometimes they change the pronunciation a bit or fiddle with the spelling, but pretty soon the word is listed in an English dictionary. Investigate your own roots. What words did your ancestors contribute to the English language? Feel free to make more than one list if you have a multicultural background! Make a note of the dictionary or book where you found the origin of each word.

INVENTION

Phydough

What! You can't pronounce this title? It's *Fido.* It's just spelled by different rules. Because English has borrowed so many words from other languages, spelling can be confusing. Take advantage of the situation! Invent new ways to spell a few words. Your inventions *must* follow an acknowledged pattern of spelling.

HISTORY

The Mystery Man

Who was William Caxton, and what did he have to do with spelling? Do a little research, and find out. Then, give a short speech or write a few pages explaining his relationship to spelling rules.

REAL LIFE

Bakers and Forrests

How did we get last names, anyway? We didn't always have them, so where did they come from? What circumstances or events made them seem necessary? Fill your classmates in on the story. While you're at it, find out what your own last name means and a few other surnames, too.

DISCUSSION

Move Over, Webster

You've been reading and writing for a lot of years now. You probably have a few of your own opinions about spelling. What are they? Discuss them with a group of friends. Listen to their ideas, too. Then, together, come up with your own new and improved spelling guide for the English language.

REAL-LIFE EXAMPLES

Candid Camera

If you've got a camera and a sense of humor, here's the project for you! Go on a photo scavenger hunt for misspelled signs. Unfortunately for English but fortunately for you, you'll find them everywhere, especially on vehicles sporting hand-painted messages and on business marquees. Of course, some of these misspellings are intentional. Go ahead and snap them, too. They'll help fill up the scrapbook you make for the class to peruse.

Proofreading Application: Poster

Good writers are generally good proofreaders. Readers tend to admire and trust writing that is error-free. Make sure that you correct all errors in grammar, usage, spelling, and punctuation in your writing. Your readers will have more confidence in your words if you have done your best to proofread carefully.

Using correct spelling is especially important in writing that will be put before the public. No matter what you are writing, every minute that you spend running a spellchecker, consulting a dictionary, and proofreading your paper adds to your credibility.

Proofreading Activity

In the following poster, find the errors in spelling and correct them using proofreading symbols in the chart on page 935 of *Elements of Language* to replace incorrect words.

Example Do you like writeing?

Come to our 1st meeting!

Franklin Junior High Writers Club

Meet the principle contributor to the popular book *Writing Made Easy.*

Mr. Daniel Gillette is an experienced writer who has published articles in numerous magazines. He will be lecturing on journals and giving advise to beginning writers. Mr. Gillette's lecture will be followed by punch and desert.

Refreshments will be free too everyone attending.

Meet us right here in Room Two hundred fifty-seven at 6:30 P.M. on Friday, November 1!

See Your Name in Print!

We will be publishing our own magazine, which is named *Cameo Appearrances.* 15 poems and stories have already been accepted for the inaugural edition.

Send submissions to Lance Ward. (Photoes and drawings will also be considered.)

Literary Model: Play

Quince. *Is all our company here?*
Bottom. *You were best to call them generally, man by man, according to the scrip.*
Quince. *Here is the scroll of every man's name, which thought fit, through all Athens, to play in our interlude before the duke and duchess, on his wedding day at night.*

Bottom. *Let me play the lion, too. I will roar that I will do any man's heart good to hear me. I will roar, that I will make the duke say, "Let him roar again, let him roar again."*
Quince. *An you should do it too terribly, you would fright the duchess and the ladies, that they would shriek; and that were enough to hang us all.*
All. *That would hang us, every mother's son.*
Bottom. *I grant you, friends, if you should fright the ladies out of their wits, they would have no more discretion buy to hang us: but I will aggravate my voice so that I will roar you as gently as any sucking dove; I will roar you as 'twere any nightingale.*

Bottom. *We will meet; and there we may rehearse most obscenely and courageously. Take pains; be perfit: adieu.*

Bottom. *Masters, you ought to consider with yourselves. To bring in—God shield us!—a lion among ladies is a dreadful thing. For there is not a more fearful wild fowl than your lion living; and we ought to look to't.*
Snout. *Therefore another prologue must tell he is not a lion.*

Bottom. *Nay, you must name his name, and half his face must be seen through the lion's neck, and he himself must speak through, saying thus, or to the same defect—"Ladies"—or, "Fair ladies—I would wish you"—or, "I would request you"—or, "I would entreat you—not to fear, not to tremble: my life for yours. If you think I come hither as a lion, it were pity of my life. No, I am no such thing. I am a man as other men are."*

—from *A Midsummer Night's Dream* by William Shakespeare
(act 1, scene 2 and act 3, scene 1)

EXERCISE A As you can see from the preceding examples, Bottom often confuses words that sound alike or have related meanings. Judging from the context of each underlined word, choose the word that Bottom meant to say.

exaggerate	seemly	genuinely	serenely
effect	individually	affect	moderate

1. generally ______________ **2.** aggravate ______________

3. obscenely ______________ **4.** defect ______________

Literary Model (continued)

EXERCISE B How does Shakespeare characterize Bottom by having him confuse words?

EXERCISE C Write a short skit in which three students make plans to perform together in a school talent show. One student tries to take charge of the performance by using fancy words but ends up using the wrong ones. Use the **Words Often Confused** list in your textbook to help you find examples of words this would-be director might (mis)use.

EXERCISE D

1. What words did the student in your skit confuse for each other?

2. How did the confusion of these words affect the meaning of what he or she was trying to say?

Writing Application: Business Letter

When the language is English, learning to spell correctly is no easy task. Unlike some languages in which a relatively simple sound-to-letter correspondence exists, English has an impressive number of words whose spelling seems to scorn any set of logical rules—take *though* and *scissors* and *rhythm* as examples. Rules that can help you improve your spelling do exist. You can also progress toward mastery by simply memorizing the spelling of the most commonly misspelled words.

It may not be quite as important to spell every word accurately when you're writing in a journal that only you will see, or when you're taking notes whose content will be revised and proofread several times before it appears in a finished document. However, anything you write that will be read by others should be free of spelling errors—including, of course, letters to potential employers in which first impressions are crucial.

Writing Activity

You are seeking an internship at a real or imaginary company or business. Write a letter to the person in charge of interns. Discuss the type of position you would like and why you would be a good candidate, including your relevant academic and work experience. Use at least five words from the spelling lists and at least five words from the lists of words that are often confused.

PREWRITING Decide the type of internship you will request in your letter. Brainstorm to create a list of qualifications. Think about your interests, hobbies, and other leisure-time activities, as well as academic coursework and previous jobs. Then, brainstorm a list of ways that your serving as an intern could benefit the company. Order the items in each list from most to least significant, from the perspective of the person who hires interns.

WRITING Begin your letter by clearly explaining your purpose and the type of internship you are seeking. Then, using your notes, write one paragraph about your qualifications and another paragraph that addresses how the company will benefit from your internship. Conclude by thanking the person for his or her time and by requesting an interview.

REVISING Read your draft to determine whether you have expressed yourself clearly, succinctly, and in standard formal English. Ask yourself if there are other qualifications you have or ways the company will benefit that you could include in the letter. You may want to have an adult look at your draft to see whether you have successfully promoted yourself. Be sure that you have used at least five words from the spelling lists and at least five words from the lists of words that are often confused.

PUBLISHING Try proofreading your letter beginning with the bottom line and moving to the top. This will help you concentrate on locating errors in spelling, grammar, and punctuation rather than on the content. In class, form job-search committees and read through a selection of letters of application. Finally, conduct mock interviews to find the best candidate for the job.

Extending Your Writing

Add this letter to the anthology you are maintaining of your best writing. You may want to refer to this letter in the future when you really are seeking employment or an internship.

Choices: Learning More About Common Errors

The following activities challenge you to find a connection between common errors and the world around you. Do the activity below that suits your personality best, and then share your discoveries with your class.

DRAMA

A Comedy of Errors

Now that you've heard the whole sad story of English errors, you've probably noticed that errors are sometimes funny. Have you also noticed that certain errors can be used for characterization? For instance, sentence fragments can characterize a scatterbrained person—someone who never finishes a thought. For this activity, write a comedy sketch. Include at least one character who makes as many language errors as possible. For contrast, have at least one character who never makes an error. Plan your sketch so that everyone is friends in the end. Then, perform your sketch for the class.

DISCUSSION

Why, Oh, Why?

The name of this chapter is "Correcting Common Errors." The errors that appear in it certainly are common. Why do these errors appear so frequently, even among the best writers? Under what circumstances might some of these errors be considered artistic or at least acceptable? Cut strips out of a big sheet of paper. Each strip should be large enough for one sentence written with a marker. Then, have everyone write down one reason for each error. Collect the strips, and use them as a springboard for discussion.

WRITING

Taking Stock

Write a letter to your teacher that tells him or her how this class has helped you understand English better. Identify the specific areas that are no longer a problem for you as well as the things that particularly interested you. It would be nice if you took special care proofreading this document.

DISCUSSION

Cold Feet

Like it or not, almost any kind of success in life requires at least a minimal ability to speak and write well. Yet, there are some people who just plain have cold feet when it comes to writing or speaking to people they don't know. Lead your class in a discussion about the feelings that make people nervous about writing or speaking. Also, discuss the feelings that enable other people to do so with ease. Then, brainstorm ways to overcome any obstacles to successful communication.

SURVEY

Pet Peeves

Although few people are experts at usage and mechanics, just about everybody has an opinion about what the worst type of error is. For some it's spelling, for others it's sentence fragments, and for others it's incorrect pronoun references. Do you have a pet peeve? Take a survey of your classmates and teachers. Ask your parents, neighbors, and relatives, too. After collecting your data, look for patterns. Do many people abhor a certain type of error? Write up your findings, and share them with your class.

RESEARCH

Past, Present, Future

Already, there are computer programs that can understand what you say and type it for you! Do you think these programs will become popular? Will most computers of the future be programmed for voice recognition? Do some research on voice-recognition programs to find out what functions they can perform today, and present your findings to your class.

Proofreading Application: Letter

Good writers are generally good proofreaders. Readers tend to admire and trust writing that is error-free. Make sure that you correct all errors in grammar, usage, spelling, and punctuation in your writing. Your readers will have more confidence in your words if you have done your best to proofread carefully.

Errors are stumbling blocks to your reader. They make writing hard to understand. Avoiding errors is especially important when you are writing to a person who may not have a full command of the English language. Letters to children or to people who are learning English should be especially clear and easy to understand. Be courteous; proofread these letters very carefully.

Proofreading Activity

In the following letter to a nonnative speaker of English, find the common errors in usage and mechanics and correct them using proofreading symbols such as those on page 935 of *Elements of Language*. You may need to rewrite some sentences. If a numbered item is correct, write *C* above it.

Example Dear Gretchen:

[1] Hi! I'm Wendy. Me and my family are so happy that you are coming to stay with us. **[2]** I'll tell you a little about our home. **[3]** You'll be sharing a room with my sister Tara and I. **[4]** Don't worry; its a big yellow room, and there's plenty of space for everyone. **[5]** You're bed is right by a window, so you can see the street. **[6]** The school that you will be attending. Only five blocks from our house, so we will walk to school together in the morning. **[7]** We have a black and white dog named Patches, our cat is named Peanut. **[8]** They are very freindly and like everyone. **[9]** Well, actually Peanut likes everyone accept Uncle Ed. **[10]** Write to us soon, and tell us when you will arrive so that we can meet you at the airport! Everyone can't hardly wait to see you!

Sincerely,

Wendy Days

Literary Model: Sentence Fragments in a Description

The black stove, stoked with coal and firewood, glows like a lighted pumpkin. Eggbeaters whirl, spoons spin round in bowls of butter and sugar, vanilla sweetens the air, ginger spices it; melting, nose-tingling odors saturate the kitchen, suffuse the house, drift out to the world on puffs of chimney smoke. In four days the work is done. Thirty-one cakes, dampened with whiskey, bask on window sills and shelves.

Who are they for?

Friends. Not necessarily neighbor friends: Indeed, the larger share are intended for persons we've met maybe once, perhaps not at all. People who've struck our fancy. Like President Roosevelt. Like the Reverend and Mrs. J. C. Lucey, Baptist missionaries to Borneo who lectured here last winter. Or the little knife grinder who comes through town twice a year. . . . Or the Young Wistons, a California couple whose car one afternoon broke down outside the house and who spent a pleasant hour chatting with us on the porch (young Mr. Wiston snapped our picture, the only one we've ever had taken). Is it because my friend is shy with everyone *except* strangers that these strangers, and merest acquaintances, seem to us our truest friends? I think yes. Also, the scrapbooks we keep of thank-you's on White House stationery, time-to-time communications from California and Borneo, the knife grinder's penny postcards, make us feel connected to eventful worlds beyond the kitchen with its views of a sky that stops.

—from "A Christmas Memory" by Truman Capote

EXERCISE A Truman Capote's description of the people to whom Buddy (the narrator) and his friend send Christmas fruitcakes is written mostly in sentence fragments. In the passage above, underline all the sentence fragments.

EXERCISE B

1. Why do you think Capote uses sentence fragments rather than complete sentences in this passage?

____

____

2. If the passage were rewritten to include only complete sentences, how would it sound different?

____

____

Literary Model (continued)

EXERCISE C Write a brief description of your own or an imaginary character's preparations for a holiday or celebration. Experiment with using sentence fragments in your description.

EXERCISE D

1. Look back over your passage. What sentence fragments did you use?

2. How did the sentence fragments you used affect the tone, voice, and style of the description?

Writing Application: Pamphlet

Good writers do not capitalize words arbitrarily. They capitalize them as an indication to the reader that they are referring to a title; starting a new sentence; or referring to a specific person, place, or thing. In some cases, whether a word is capitalized or not changes the meaning of a sentence. Compare these sentences:

Spend some time at hot springs before leaving Arkansas.

Spend some time at Hot Springs before leaving Arkansas.

Writing Activity

Have you ever heard people lamenting that the only time they visit places of interest in their own town or city is when they're taking out-of-town guests there? Many of us are more familiar with the special attractions and areas of a city five hundred miles away than with those close to our own backyard. You've decided to get to know your town or city much better so that you'll be the perfect guide the next time your relatives come to visit. You're going to take a real or imaginary tour through parts of your town or city and jot down notes about your route and what you see. Then, you'll use these notes to create a pamphlet about your discoveries that your future visitors can enjoy. Since you'll be mentioning the names of buildings, sites, and perhaps historical figures, remember to capitalize all proper nouns and titles as needed.

PREWRITING Decide how you will arrange your ideas. You may prefer to think in spatial terms—for example, beginning with places of interest in the southern part of the city and ending with places in the northern part. Alternatively, you may want to use a logical order, according to which you might categorize outdoor places, historical places, and special places for children. In addition to the arrangement of ideas, determine the tone you will adopt. The tone you use will influence your choice of words and sentence structure.

WRITING Using your notes and keeping in mind the arrangement of ideas and tone you have chosen, begin your draft. Write freely while still expressing your ideas clearly. Enhance your draft by adding sensory details that will bring to life for your reader each place of interest you're describing. As you write, visualize how the text will appear in the pamphlet.

REVISING Have a classmate read your draft of the pamphlet text. Ask him or her to imagine being an out-of-town visitor and to answer this question: Would these descriptions, intended for a pamphlet, make you want to visit these places of interest? Encourage your classmate to give you suggestions about how to further enliven the writing.

PUBLISHING As you proofread your draft, pay special attention to capitalization. Consult a dictionary if you're not sure whether to capitalize a word. Since your pamphlet is intended for people unfamiliar with the places you've mentioned, carefully check the spelling of the place names. You may choose to add pictures to your pamphlet. Make copies of the final product and pass them out to the class.

Extending Your Writing

Perhaps you could create a pamphlet using the text you've written and graphics generated by a software program. You could then collect your classmates' pamphlets and present them to the local chamber of commerce.

Section 2: Practice with Sentences and Paragraphs

NAME ______ CLASS ______ DATE ______

for **CHAPTER 18: EXERCISE 1** *page 479* **PRACTICE A, WORKSHEET 1**

Identifying Sentence Fragments

DIRECTIONS Some of the following items are sentence fragments. To find out which items are fragments and which are complete sentences, apply the three-part test on page 478 of your textbook.

- If the item is a complete sentence, write C next to the item number.
- If a subject is missing, write *S*.
- If a verb is missing, write *V*.
- If the item has a subject and verb but does not express a complete thought, write *N*.

______ **1.** An important step in growing up is learning to accept imperfections in yourself and others.

______ **2.** Since no human being can be perfect.

______ **3.** My brother Luis has never learned this lesson.

______ **4.** Is quick to notice other people's faults.

______ **5.** He also extremely critical of himself.

______ **6.** After we tell Luis his carvings are great.

______ **7.** Replies that they are not really good enough.

______ **8.** The way that he sees them in his mind.

______ **9.** Because the carving on one bookend didn't match the other.

______ **10.** Threw them both out.

______ **11.** Made a wooden box but hid it because of a small scratch.

______ **12.** Luis is not happy much of the time.

______ **13.** Is a perfectionist overcome by unimportant flaws.

______ **14.** Luis miserable but doesn't need to be.

______ **15.** Should understand that even experts make mistakes.

______ **16.** The computer software designer whose program crashed.

______ **17.** The big-league pitcher who threw four straight balls to the weakest hitter on the other team.

______ **18.** The designer and the pitcher moved on.

______ **19.** If he could realize.

______ **20.** Should not be overwhelmed by minor shortcomings along the way.

Identifying Sentence Fragments

DIRECTIONS Some of the following items are sentence fragments. To find out which items are fragments and which are complete sentences, apply the three-part test on page 478 of your textbook.

- If the item is a complete sentence, write C next to the item number.
- If a subject is missing, write *S*.
- If a verb is missing, write *V*.
- If the item has a subject and verb but does not express a complete thought, write *N*.

______ **1.** Members of my family pursue interesting hobbies.

______ **2.** Enjoy collecting old books, growing rare flowers, and knitting hot pads.

______ **3.** Uncle Raymond writing and performing country music.

______ **4.** Carries his audio recorders everywhere.

______ **5.** First ideas just a word or phrase or part of a melody.

______ **6.** Always listens to country stations while driving to find out what kinds of songs are most popular.

______ **7.** Although only one of Raymond's songs has been on the charts.

______ **8.** Still spends most of his free time songwriting and cutting demos to send to recording studios.

______ **9.** Love the catchy melodies of his songs.

______ **10.** The family often asks Raymond to perform.

______ **11.** Brings his electric guitar and piles of sheet music.

______ **12.** Sometimes sing along and dance, and the time flies.

______ **13.** Helping Raymond make a demo at a recording studio, however, not always a pleasure.

______ **14.** Knowing exactly how the songs should sound.

______ **15.** Raymond often critical of session players, especially drummers.

______ **16.** He believes rhythm is key to the impact of a song.

______ **17.** Fresh word combinations very important, too.

______ **18.** Sometimes need to discuss Raymond's song in detail.

______ **19.** So all the musicians will be on the same wavelength.

______ **20.** When everything works together.

Revising Phrase Fragments

DIRECTIONS Create sentences from the following phrases. You can either (1) attach the fragment to a complete sentence, or (2) develop the phrase into a complete sentence by adding a subject, a verb, or both.

1. about her weekly schedule

2. riding her new bicycle

3. to fish for rainbow trout

4. eating breakfast

5. two tests on the same day

6. to prepare a salad

7. beyond the last gasoline station

8. one of the Great Lakes

9. crossing the mountains

10. to explore the river valley

11. walking along the beach at sunset

12. to become a great athlete

Revising Phrase Fragments

DIRECTIONS Create sentences from the following phrases. You can either (1) attach the fragment to a complete sentence, or (2) develop the phrase into a complete sentence by adding a subject, a verb, or both.

1. memorizing the song

2. on an exciting trip

3. checking the car for dents

4. on a ranch in Colorado

5. the only beach open to the public

6. to see great distances

7. during the ninth inning

8. a South American country

9. beside the castle ruins

10. to get a free ticket

11. the best meal of the day

12. during the first half of the game

Revising Subordinate Clause Fragments

DIRECTIONS The following paragraphs contain some subordinate clause fragments.

- Find and underline the clause fragments.
- Revise the paragraphs, joining the subordinate clauses with the independent clauses. (There may be more than one way to join them.)
- Change the punctuation and capitalization as necessary.

EXAMPLE The Galápagos are isolated islands, ~~W~~hich have unique wildlife.

1. The Galápagos Islands lie in the Pacific Ocean around 600 miles west of mainland Ecuador. Which governs them. About 10,000 people live there. Although the islands have active volcanoes. Because the Galápagos are isolated. They are home to unusual species of plants and animals. There is not much variety in species, however. Because the islands lie far from the mainland. One of the longest-living creatures on Earth is the giant land tortoise. Which lives only in the Galápagos. Other animals include the flightless cormorant and the swimming marine iguana, which feeds on seaweed.

2. Passenger planes were very uncomfortable. Before aerospace technology improved dramatically in the 1930s. Biplanes, aircraft with two wings (one above the other) and an open cockpit, were built around a metal framework. That was covered with cloth or sometimes plywood. The passenger compartment typically contained wicker chairs. Which were not attached to the floor. Because the planes were noisy. Passengers had to wear earplugs. They also usually needed warm clothing. When the pressurized cabin was developed in the late 1930s. Faster flights became possible, since planes could fly higher. Where there was less air turbulence.

Revising Subordinate Clause Fragments

DIRECTIONS The following paragraphs contain some subordinate clause fragments.

- Find and underline the clause fragments.
- Revise the paragraphs, joining the subordinate clauses with the independent clauses. (There may be more than one way to join them.)
- Change the punctuation and capitalization as necessary.

EXAMPLE While we were cleaning my grandmother's attic, we found a box of old buttons.

1. Buttons have been used for thousands of years. They originated in South Asia around 2000 B.C. as decorative items for clothing. Buttons made of shells were found. When archaeologists were digging in the Indus Valley of present-day Pakistan. The ancient Greeks used buttons and loops to fasten their tunics. Although buttonholes were not invented in Europe until the thirteenth century. They are very common today. By the fourteenth century, buttons adorned many garments. Because they were beautiful and could indicate a person's wealth. In 1520, the king of France ordered a black velvet suit with 13,400 gold buttons. Because he wanted to impress the English king. Today, some people collect old buttons.

2. Carnivores are mammals. That eat mostly meat. The majority of carnivores are fast moving and agile. Their eyes are forward facing. Which helps them judge distance when hunting. Their teeth have developed to excel at cutting flesh. Most mammals have two long, sharp teeth in the top jaw and two in the bottom jaw called canine teeth. They also have molars for chewing. While the big cats eat meat. They do little chewing. Their stomachs have especially strong digestive chemicals. Although bear, badger, and fox hunt other animals. They also eat plants.

Using Subordinate Clauses in Sentences

DIRECTIONS Use each of the subordinate clause fragments as part of a complete sentence.

- Add whatever words are necessary to make the meaning of the sentence complete.
- Add words to the beginning or to the end of the fragments.
- Add capitalization and punctuation as necessary.
- Make your changes on the worksheet.

1. after Robert cooked dinner

2. who was very hungry

3. when his dog started barking

4. after he heard a knock at the door

5. that it startled him

6. when he finally decided to answer

7. who was at the door

8. because he was thinking about the movie he was watching

9. which was pretty scary

10. after Robert watched the movie

11. as he shut off the lights

12. if he ever saw that movie again

Using Subordinate Clauses in Sentences

DIRECTIONS Use each of the subordinate clause fragments as part of a complete sentence.

- Add whatever words are necessary to make the meaning of the sentence complete.
- Add words to the beginning or to the end of the fragments.
- Add capitalization and punctuation as necessary.
- Make your changes on the worksheet.

1. because Lisa's math homework was more difficult than she had expected

2. since she needed to break in her new running shoes

3. which were constructed with special soles

4. when she began the run

5. as soon as she reached the first steep incline

6. while at the top of the hill

7. after she descended the hill

8. when she reached the bridge over the river

9. because the sun was setting

10. soon after she returned home

11. that the new shoes were great

12. although she had saved her allowance for three months

Identifying and Revising Fragments

DIRECTIONS Some of the following groups of words are sentence fragments.

- Draw a line under each fragment, and make it part of a complete sentence, changing punctuation and capitals where necessary.
- When you find a complete sentence, write *C* on the line provided.

EXAMPLE The ones you find on the beach are usually dead, washed onto the sand and stranded.

_____ **1.** There are about 1,800 kinds of starfish. Which in fact are not fish because they have no backbone.

_____ **2.** Starfish live at the bottom of the sea. Usually have arms surrounding a disk. And average eight to twelve inches across.

_____ **3.** Many starfish have suction-tube feet. Which help them move or hold on to steep surfaces.

_____ **4.** Most starfish feed on tiny organic matter. Although some eat clams.

_____ **5.** When eating a clam. A starfish uses its suction feet to open the shell, then pushes its stomach out of its mouth and into the shell.

_____ **6.** Starfish typically have five hollow arms, but some have 19 or more arms.

_____ **7.** At the end of each starfish arm is a light-sensitive spot, a kind of simple eye.

_____ **8.** If a starfish loses an arm. It grows a new one.

_____ **9.** Starfish move very slowly. And usually prey on even slower creatures.

_____ **10.** Because the big crown-of-thorns starfish eats coral polyps. Large numbers of them can destroy coral reefs.

Identifying and Revising Fragments

DIRECTIONS Some of the following groups of words are sentence fragments.

- Draw a line under each fragment, and make it part of a complete sentence, changing punctuation and capitals where necessary.
- When you find a complete sentence, write *C* on the line provided.

EXAMPLE Because we take common articles of clothing for granted, we often are unaware of their history.

______ **1.** Rubber-soled athletic shoes are called sneakers. Because people can walk very quietly—sneak—in them.

______ **2.** Even before 1900. Rubber was used for the soles of leather-topped shoes.

______ **3.** In 1839 Charles Goodyear discovered vulcanization. Which, by adding sulfur to rubber, makes it elastic over a much greater range of temperatures.

______ **4.** Because brown was a popular shoe color. Early sneakers featured brown canvas tops.

______ **5.** Sneakers made in Japan became popular in the 1960s. Since they were lightweight.

______ **6.** By putting a piece of rubber into a waffle iron, famous University of Oregon track coach Bill Bowerman created the waffle sole pattern.

______ **7.** Proving to be more breathable. Nylon fabric was later used for sneaker tops.

______ **8.** Today, shoe companies sell sneakers by appealing to our appreciation of colors. Our love for innovative designs, and our admiration of famous athletes.

______ **9.** They seem to say that their brand will make us into talented athletes.

______ **10.** You need athletic ability, however. And sneakers alone can't transform you.

Revising Run-on Sentences

DIRECTIONS The following items are confusing because they are run-on sentences. Clear up the confusion by revising the run-ons to form clear, complete sentences. Use the method given in parentheses after each sentence.

EXAMPLE Our dog tries to wrestle with our cat; however, the cat usually wins. (Use a semicolon and a conjunctive adverb.)

1. Jules ran into the woods no one could find him for hours. (Use a comma and a coordinating conjunction.)

2. The reporters waited outside, the girl told her story inside the school. (Use a semicolon and a conjunctive adverb.)

3. The jacket was unusual it was made of satin and leather. (Make two sentences.)

4. I want to mail this letter, I don't have any postage stamps. (Use a comma and a coordinating conjunction.)

5. Ellen wanted to go to the movie she stayed home and completed her homework. (Use a semicolon and a conjunctive adverb.)

6. There were ten messages on the telephone answering machine, they were all for me. (Make two sentences.)

7. New York City has many wonderful museums the Metropolitan Museum of Art is one of the world's greatest. (Use a semicolon.)

8. Chaim doesn't like going to the dentist he knows it's important. (Use a comma and a coordinating conjunction.)

Revising Run-on Sentences

DIRECTIONS The following items are confusing because they are run-on sentences. Clear up the confusion by revising the run-ons to form clear, complete sentences. Use the method given in parentheses after each sentence.

EXAMPLE The Ojibwa are also known as the Chippewa they are one of many Algonquian-speaking peoples. (Make two sentences.)

1. Ojibwa live in the present-day United States, they also live in present-day Canada. (Use a semicolon.)

2. In the nineteenth century, the Ojibwa lived along the north shore of Lake Huron they also lived along the shores of Lake Superior. (Use a semicolon.)

3. The Ojibwa collected wild rice they also grew corn and fished. (Use a comma and a coordinating conjunction.)

4. Canoes were important modes of Ojibwa transportation they were made of birch bark. (Make two sentences.)

5. The Ojibwa also used birch bark for utensils and for wigwams birch trees were plentiful. (Make two sentences.)

6. Toboggans provided transport in winter snowshoes were also used. (Use a semicolon.)

7. There was no overall leader of the Ojibwa local leaders sometimes achieved considerable power through dealings with European fur traders. (Use a semicolon and a conjunctive adverb.)

8. Today, the Ojibwa are one of the largest groups of American Indians they number about 30,000 in the United States and about 50,000 in Canada. (Use a semicolon.)

Revising Fragments and Run-on Sentences

DIRECTIONS The following paragraphs contain several sentence fragments and run-on sentences.

- Underline the fragments once and the run-ons twice.
- Revise the paragraphs to eliminate the fragments and correct the run-ons, adding words and changing the punctuation and capitalization as necessary to make each sentence clear and complete.

1. In history class we are studying Egypt the ancient Egyptians had many fascinating customs. Some pharaohs built huge structures. These pyramids intended as tombs. After a pharaoh died, the body was embalmed it was then placed in an inner chamber of the pyramid. Along with many articles for the afterlife. These articles included furniture and clothing. Often the walls of the chamber were inscribed with passages. From the *Book of the Dead,* a collection of many texts. These inscriptions were believed to help the pharaoh overcome dangers in the afterlife.

2. To my mother's dismay. My younger brother Salvador finds her stamp collection intriguing more than once, Salvador has mailed a letter with a valuable stamp that our mother had saved. If Mother were not determined to collect stamps with pictures of animals, I'm sure that Salvador would have reformed long ago, unfortunately, animal stamps are Mother's specialty, they are also Salvador's favorites. Salvador most interested in tropical birds. If Salvador does not learn to keep his hands off Mother's stamps. I fear she will lock them in a safe place. Then, he not be able to enjoy them anymore.

Revising Fragments and Run-on Sentences

DIRECTIONS The following paragraphs contain several sentence fragments and run-on sentences.

- Underline the fragments once and the run-ons twice.
- Revise the paragraphs to eliminate the fragments and correct the run-ons, adding words and changing the punctuation and capitalization as necessary to make each sentence clear and complete.

1. Monticello, the historic home of Thomas Jefferson, the third President of the United States. Welcomes hundreds of thousands of tourists each year. The home is located in Virginia, near Charlottesville. A French baron one of many visitors during Jefferson's lifetime. The baron, who visited in 1816, was especially fascinated by Jefferson's collection he wrote an account of what he saw. Included a mammoth's jaw, an elephant's tusk, a buffalo hide with a battle scene, and a peace pipe. He also saw a map of the famous Lewis and Clark expedition. From St. Louis. To the Pacific Ocean. Visitors to Monticello today also find Jefferson's collection fascinating, many of the rare items that were at Monticello in 1816 are still on display.

2. To stay healthy. You need to eat a balanced diet. Carbohydrates, fats, and proteins are the main ingredients of a balanced diet a healthful diet also includes small amounts of other substances. Called vitamins and minerals. Vitamins help bring about chemical changes in your body. Because vitamins have long chemical names. They are commonly known by letters such as A, B, C, D, and E. Important minerals include iron, sodium, calcium, potassium, chloride, and iodine. You also small amounts of other minerals such as copper and zinc. A well-balanced diet can supply all the vitamins and minerals. Needed for good health.

Combining by Inserting Words

DIRECTIONS Combine each set of the following sentences. Some words have been italicized to help you.

- Insert the italicized word (or words) into the first sentence.
- The directions in parentheses tell you when a word form should be changed.
- Make all changes on the worksheet, using a caret (∧) to insert words.

EXAMPLE On June 30, 1908, there was a mysterious explosion in the ∧ night sky over northern Russia. ~~It happened at *night*.~~

1. An object exploded above Earth. The object was *mysterious*. (Change *An* to *A*.)
2. People as far as five hundred miles away heard a sound. It was like *thunder*. (Add *–ing* to *thunder*.)
3. The night skies in Europe were so bright that people could take photographs without a flash. This was in *northern* Europe.
4. Eyewitnesses saw colors that looked like a rainbow. They were *startled*.
5. A Russian scientist finally reached the site in 1927. The site was in a *remote* area.
6. The scientist, Leonid Kulik, searched for evidence that would explain what had caused the devastation in the area. He was unsuccessful. (Add *–ly* to *unsuccessful*.)
7. Kulik found an area of fallen trees, all pointing away from a spot. The spot was at the center of the area. (Change *center* to *central*.)
8. There were upright trees at the spot itself. The trees were *burned*.
9. For twelve miles around the spot, the trees pointed away from the center. The trees were *uprooted*.
10. Today, scientists think it is likely that a meteor exploded six miles above the area. It was a *giant* meteor.

Combining by Inserting Words

DIRECTIONS Combine each set of the following sentences. Some words have been italicized to help you.

- Insert the italicized word (or words) into the first sentence.
- The directions in parentheses tell you when a word form should be changed.
- Make all changes on the worksheet, using a caret (∧) to insert words.

EXAMPLE Henry Ford, a technological genius, helped create an industry that changed American culture.
~~*Henry Ford was a technological genius.*~~

1. Henry Ford was born in 1863 on his family's farm near Dearborn. Dearborn is in *Michigan.*

2. Ford left the farm in 1879 to go to Detroit. This was a wise move. (Add *–ly* to *wise.*)

3. In Detroit, he found work in shops. They were *machine* shops.

4. When he returned to the family farm, he made a tractor he called a farm locomotive. The tractor used *steam power.* (Add *–ed* to *power* and a hyphen following *steam.*)

5. In 1893, Ford took a position at the Detroit Edison Company. He was an *engineer.* (Add *–ing* to *engineer,* and change *a* to *an.*)

6. He did not have to work regular hours, so he had plenty of time to experiment. This was *lucky.* (Change *lucky* to *luckily* and place a comma after it.)

7. Ford started the Ford Motor Company in 1903 with support from a group of ordinary citizens. They gave him *financial* support.

8. He developed a technique for assembling cars. Assembling was *quick* and *efficient.* (Add *–ly* to *quick* and to *efficient.*)

9. This technique was called mass production. It was a *new* way of making things.

10. Through his company, Ford contributed to major changes in the United States. These changes affected both *society* and the *economy.* (Change *society* to *social* and *economy* to *economic.*)

Combining by Inserting Words

DIRECTIONS Combine the following pairs of sentences by deciding which words to insert. Remember that there may be more than one way to combine each pair of sentences.

- Choose the combination you think is best.
- Change the forms of words as necessary.
- Make all changes on the worksheet, using a caret (^) to insert words.

EXAMPLE Juana's family planned to spend a ^week-long summer vacation on Florida's east coast. ~~They planned a week-long vacation.~~

1. A week before the trip, Juana watched a movie about sharks. Movies about sharks terrify her.
2. How could she get rid of her fear of sharks? The fear nagged at her.
3. Juana decided to gather information about sharks at the library. She wanted to know about sharks in detail.
4. Ms. Ying, her teacher, directed her to some Internet sites. The sites were reliable.
5. Juana learned that sharks' skeletons are made of something instead of bones. Their skeletons are made of cartilage.
6. Because they have no swim bladder to keep them afloat, sharks have to swim. Their swimming is constant.
7. Sharks search for food mostly by using their sense of smell. Their sense of smell is keen.
8. Crisscrossing as they feed, sharks can get into a frenzy and attack one another. The crisscrossing is rapid.
9. On some beaches, lifeguards watch for sharks from structures. The structures look like towers.
10. Juana learned that there are about one hundred shark attacks on people every year. This is the final fact that Juana found.

Combining by Inserting Words

DIRECTIONS Combine the following pairs of sentences by deciding which words to insert. Remember that there may be more than one way to combine each pair of sentences.

- Choose the combination you think is best.
- Change the forms of words as necessary.
- Make all changes on the worksheet, using a caret (∧) to insert words.

EXAMPLE Antarctica is ~~one~~ [the most remote] of Earth's seven continents. ~~It is the most remote continent.~~

1. The fifth largest continent, Antarctica is located at the South Pole. It surrounds the South Pole.
2. The area of the continent doubles in winter. Sea ice forms at its edges.
3. In 1983, Antarctica had a low temperature of –128.6°F (–89.2°C). It was a record.
4. The waters around Antarctica are home to whales. Seals and penguins live there, too.
5. Krill are part of the sea life at Antarctica. Krill are tiny and shrimplike.
6. A sailing expedition circled Antarctica in 1819–1821. The Russians sailed around the continent.
7. Later explorers realized that the land at the South Pole was a continent. The land there always has a cover of ice.
8. Antarctica has no native human population, but groups of scientists live there. The scientists' support staff lives there, too.
9. Because it is so isolated, psychological and sleep studies are conducted in Antarctica. The studies are frequent.
10. Antarctica is believed to have large deposits of oil. Large deposits of natural gas are also thought to exist in Antarctica.

Combining by Inserting Phrases

DIRECTIONS Revise each of the following sets of sentences to create one sentence. There may be more than one way to combine the sentences.

- In numbers 1 through 5, the words you need to insert are italicized.
- In numbers 6 through 10, change the forms of words or omit words as indicated in parentheses, and add commas where they are needed.
- Make all changes on the worksheet.

EXAMPLE

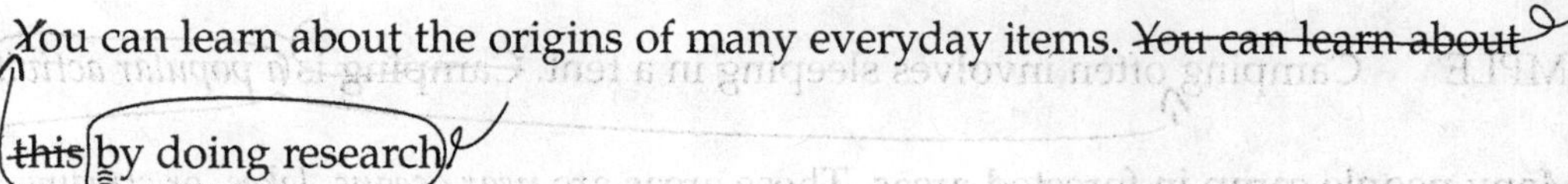

1. Karen received a piggy bank as a birthday present. She got it *from her older sister.*

2. Karen was curious. She was curious *about the origin of piggy banks.*

3. She wondered why the money container wasn't named after the squirrel. The squirrel is *known for saving food.*

4. Karen found a book about the origins of common objects. She was looking *in the library.*

5. In the Middle Ages, many people kept their savings in their houses. They kept the money *in small jars.*

6. These jars were made of pygg. Pygg was a cheap and widely used clay. (Omit *Pygg was.*)

7. People called them pygg jars. The jars later became known as pig banks. (Omit *The jars* and *became.*)

8. English potters started making banks in the shape of pigs. This was during the eighteenth century. (Omit *This was.*)

9. Today's piggy banks come in all shapes, colors, and styles. They are made of clay as well as other materials. (Omit *They are.*)

10. Karen read the rest of the book. She was fascinated by the origins of other objects. (Omit *She was.*)

Combining by Inserting Phrases

DIRECTIONS Revise each of the following sets of sentences to create one sentence. There may be more than one way to combine the sentences.

- In numbers 1 through 5, the words you need to insert are italicized.
- In numbers 6 through 10, change the forms of words or omit words as indicated in parentheses, and add commas where they are needed.
- Make all changes on the worksheet.

EXAMPLE Camping often involves sleeping in a tent. ~~Camping is~~ *a popular activity.*

1. Many people camp in forested areas. These areas are *near oceans, lakes, or streams.*
2. Camping became widespread when more people had cars to get to campsites and better camping gear was developed. This happened *after World War II.*
3. There are more than one million well-developed campsites. These campsites are *in the United States alone.*
4. Some campgrounds have showers or restaurants. These campgrounds are often *near towns or cities.*
5. Some people drive to camping areas, while others, preferring more seclusion, hike or canoe. Hikers and boaters often go *to remote areas.*
6. People who want to get far away from civilization consult topographical maps. Topographical maps show elevations, hiking trails, and water sources. (Omit *Topographical maps* and change *show* to *showing.*)
7. Some campers hike to isolated places. They carry their food and gear in backpacks. (Omit *They* and change *carry* to *carrying.*)
8. Hikers prefer lightweight tents. These weigh as little as two pounds. (Omit *These* and change *weigh* to *weighing.*)
9. Sleeping bags are also available in lightweight materials. These materials include goose down, duck down, and synthetic fibers. (Omit *These materials* and change *include* to *including.*)
10. Thomas Holding was the founder of recreational camping. Holding wrote the first handbook for campers in 1908. (Omit *Holding* and change *write* to *writing.*)

Creating Compound Subjects and Verbs

DIRECTIONS Combine each pair of the following short sentences into a single sentence.

- Make sure that each sentence has a compound subject, a compound verb, or both.
- Make sure that verbs and subjects agree in number.

1. Ping-Pong™ is one name for a popular indoor game involving a ball and paddles. Table tennis is another name for the game.

2. In the 1880s, the balls used for the game were makeshift. The paddles also were makeshift.

3. Later, celluloid balls were manufactured. Paddles called battledores were manufactured. These items were sold.

4. Parker Brothers, a game company, copyrighted the name Ping-Pong™. The company promoted the game.

5. Hungarians were the best players. Hungarian players won the first world championship in 1927.

6. A Hungarian champion toured the United States in the 1930s. He popularized the game.

7. As a result, five million American families bought Ping-Pong™ equipment. They used Ping-Pong™ equipment.

8. Players enjoy Ping-Pong™. Spectators enjoy Ping-Pong™, too. Both players and spectators find the game exciting.

9. In 1971, the American table tennis team met the Chinese team. They competed in China.

10. In 1988, singles competition for men and for women became part of the Olympic Games. In the same year, doubles competition for both sexes was added to the Olympics.

Creating Compound Subjects and Verbs

DIRECTIONS Combine each pair of the following short sentences into a single sentence.

- Make sure that each sentence has a compound subject, a compound verb, or both.
- Make sure that verbs and subjects agree in number.

1. American people were attracted to California by the promise of gold in 1848. Chinese people were also attracted to California by the promise of gold.

2. China's difficult political situation was a reason that Chinese people moved to the United States. China's poor economy was a reason that Chinese people moved to the United States.

3. Chinese immigrants prospected for gold. They later worked on the American transcontinental railroad.

4. The first Chinese arrived in San Francisco. The first Chinese opened many businesses.

5. Many non-Chinese workers feared immigrants would take jobs from them. Labor unions also feared immigrants would take jobs from them.

6. Along with other immigrants, the Chinese faced violence. They encountered discrimination.

7. During World War II the United States and China became allies. They fought against Japan.

8. San Francisco has a large Chinese American community. New York City and Honolulu have large Chinese American communities.

Combining to Create Compound Sentences

DIRECTIONS The sentences in the following pairs are closely related in meaning.

- Using the methods you have learned, combine each pair into a compound sentence.
- You may choose from coordinating conjunctions (*and, but, for, nor, so,* or *yet*), or from conjunctive adverbs (*also, anyway, consequently, however, instead, likewise, nevertheless, still, then, therefore*).
- Make all changes on the worksheet.

EXAMPLE Tom and Yusef ^were leaving ~~walked through~~ the Detroit Institute of Art, ^but ~~A~~ mural, or wall painting, by Mexican artist Diego Rivera caught their attention.

1. Tom had seen a Rivera mural in Mexico City. Tom told Yusef about Rivera.

2. Rivera was influenced by painters from other countries. His style is distinctly his own.

3. Some of Rivera's murals form narratives. His murals at the National Palace in Mexico City depict episodes in Mexican history.

4. Rivera's wife, Frida Kahlo, was a highly praised painter. She is noted for her intensely colored self-portraits.

5. Rivera is well known. José Clemente Orozco is regarded by many as the greatest Mexican muralist.

6. Orozco didn't express strong political viewpoints. His murals show his emotional reactions to the hardships of common people.

7. Orozco was born in Mexico. Many of his most famous murals are in the United States.

8. Orozco spent a lot of time in the United States. Several of his murals can be seen in New York and California.

9. Orozco is famous for his murals. He also painted on canvas.

10. Orozco was successful. He never lost his focus on the suffering of humanity.

Combining to Create Compound Sentences

DIRECTIONS The sentences in the following pairs are closely related in meaning.

- Using the methods you have learned, combine each pair into a compound sentence. Make all changes on the worksheet.
- You may choose from coordinating conjunctions (*and, but, for, nor, so,* or *yet*), or from conjunctive adverbs (*also, anyway, consequently, however, instead, likewise, nevertheless, still, then, therefore*).

EXAMPLE The hamburger is considered an American food; however, shredded meat has been popular around the world for a long time.

1. The common hamburger got its start in medieval times. Shredded meat was popular among Asian peoples known as Tartars.
2. Shredding meat made it more digestible. The Tartars shredded tough meat from their cattle.
3. By the fourteenth century, the Germans were shredding meat. They added spices to the meat and served it both raw and cooked.
4. In Hamburg the meat was called Hamburg steak. It was a popular meal for poor people.
5. In the 1800s, an English doctor named J. H. Salisbury believed that shredding food made it more digestible. He recommended that people shred all their food before eating.
6. Salisbury thought beef should be eaten three times a day. He believed it should be washed down with hot water.
7. Named after Dr. Salisbury, Salisbury steak is similar to today's hamburger. It was served on a plate, not a bun.
8. The "Hamburg steak" came to the United States with German immigrants in the 1880s. It became known as "hamburger steak."
9. It is not known just when somebody first put the meat in a bun. It was in sandwich form when it was served at the 1904 St. Louis World's Fair.
10. Today, we have many more ways to prepare food than did the Tartars. Shredded beef is still a favorite.

Combining to Create Complex Sentences

DIRECTIONS Using subordinate clauses, combine each pair of the following sentences into a single complex sentence. Remember that there may be different ways to combine the sentences. Choose the way that seems best.

- Change or delete words as necessary to make smooth combinations.

1. Caves and glaciers are endlessly fascinating. They attract explorers from all walks of life.

2. Caves are shaped by acidic water. The water trickles down through surface cracks and dissolves the rock around them.

3. Inside caves, visitors see stalactites and stalagmites. These are colorful, free-form columns.

4. The two terms are similar. It is easy to remember the difference between them.

5. Stalac*tites* hang from the ceilings of caves. They have to hold on *tight*.

6. Stalagmites are formed on the floors of caves. The minerals are deposited by dripping water.

7. Glaciers are huge masses of ice. They create landforms such as valleys and fjords.

8. Glaciers are formed from snow. The snow remains after the summer melting season and refreezes into smaller particles.

9. Glaciers contain about 75 percent of Earth's fresh water. They make up about 11 percent of Earth's surface.

10. A moving glacier collects debris. The debris can range from dust to boulders.

Combining to Create Complex Sentences

DIRECTIONS Using subordinate clauses, combine each pair of the following sentences into a single complex sentence. Remember that there may be different ways to combine the sentences. Choose the way that seems best.

- Change or delete words as necessary to make smooth combinations.

1. Laos and Cambodia are neighboring countries in Southeast Asia. They share a history of traditional and classical dancing with other countries in the area.

2. Festivals in these countries frequently accompany historical holidays. A holiday's significance is explained through rituals of music and dance.

3. Classical Laotian dances were once performed only for the king and his guests. The dances tell the story of the creation of the ancient kingdom.

4. The message of the dance is often conveyed by subtle facial expressions and delicate hand gestures. The dancers are skilled at pantomime.

5. A troupe of Laotian dancers became established in Nashville, Tennessee. The dancers wanted to preserve their art and perform in the United States.

6. Cambodian dancers have successfully revived traditional Khmer dancing. It had been inactive since the fifteenth century.

7. Roles in Khmer dance include the male, the female, the monkey, and the giant. These roles make a performance typical of Khmer dance.

8. The dance is a combination of graceful hand gestures and body movements. The movements have special meanings.

Revising a Paragraph by Combining Sentences

DIRECTIONS Using all of the sentence-combining techniques you have learned, revise the following short paragraphs. Do not change their meaning.

- Use your judgment to decide which sentences to combine and how to combine them.
- Write clear, varied sentences that read smoothly.

1. Women first played basketball in 1892. They played at Smith College. The game was introduced by Senda Berenson Abbott. She was a physical education teacher. Berenson Abbott thought the men's game was too physically demanding for women. She devised different rules. For example, players had to stay in assigned areas. Players also had to get rid of the ball after dribbling three times. Today, the rules for women's basketball are the same as those for men's. This is with a couple of minor exceptions.

2. Roger traveled to New York City to visit his aunt and uncle. His aunt and uncle were retired. His brother came along. They traveled from their home in San Francisco. For fun, they kept track of the kinds of transportation they used. They rode a bus to the cable car stop. They took the cable car to the travel agency. They took a taxi to the airport and flew to New York. In New York, they rode the subway. Then they walked from the subway to a pier. There they boarded a boat. The boat circled New York harbor. At the end of their visit, Roger was surprised. His brother was surprised, too. They had used six kinds of transportation in less than a week.

Revising a Paragraph by Combining Sentences

DIRECTIONS Using all of the sentence-combining techniques you have learned, revise the following short paragraphs. Do not change their meaning.

- Use your judgment to decide which sentences to combine and how to combine them.
- Write clear, varied sentences that read smoothly.

1. A glider is a kind of aircraft. It is very light. It has no engine. It is heavier than air. It stays up because of aerodynamic forces acting on its long, narrow wings. A good glider can fly in calm air. In calm air, it will sink less than 36 inches per second. Octave Chanute built early gliders. Orville and Wilbur Wright built early gliders, too. These three men contributed information that was used to design the first powered aircraft. These American inventors were among the early pioneers of gliders.

2. Putting on a play is hard but interesting work. All kinds of people work together. People in a play have different talents and skills. Some are actors. Some are designers. They design scenery and costumes. One person directs the play. Others control the lights. Others collect or make props. Props are the items decorating the set or used by the actors. Copies of the script must be prepared. This happens once a play is chosen. The script is the written text of the play. Everybody gets a copy of the script. The actors start learning their lines. The director decides how the actors will move on the stage. The director also offers suggestions. He or she suggests how lines should be delivered.

Revising Sentences to Create Parallel Structure

DIRECTIONS Bring balance to the following sentences by putting the ideas in parallel form.

- Write *C* if a sentence is correct.
- Add or delete words as necessary.
- Make all changes on the worksheet.

EXAMPLE ~~To be~~ Being an only child may be fun, but not having my brothers is unimaginable.

______ **1.** Marco loves singing, acting, and to play the drums.

______ **2.** Jeremy eats lunch in the cafeteria, at home, or he goes to a restaurant.

______ **3.** During the speech, the governor showed that she has vision, confidence, and is ambitious.

______ **4.** The teacher suggested that we hold a concert and make a music videotape.

______ **5.** Meeting voters, answering questions, and discussion of community issues are important aspects of political campaigning.

______ **6.** Persuading my mother to let me go will be hard, but to talk my father into it will be even harder.

______ **7.** Because he has confidence and being naturally graceful, Tyrone will be a good gymnast.

______ **8.** The collection in our public library is better than the collections in many college libraries.

______ **9.** Olivia took a lot of time doing the research and to write the report.

______ **10.** Losing the soccer game was difficult, but knowing that they played hard and improving their teamwork helped them feel better.

______ **11.** In her speech, Eva discussed the importance of empathy, forgiveness, and being kind.

______ **12.** Leon persuaded the student council to seek funding for a Japanese class and to ask for healthier lunches.

NAME ______ CLASS ______ DATE ______

for **CHAPTER 19: EXERCISE 7** *page 498* **PRACTICE B, WORKSHEET 30**

Revising Sentences to Create Parallel Structure

DIRECTIONS Bring balance to the following sentences by putting the ideas in parallel form.

- Write C if a sentence is correct.
- Add or delete words as necessary.
- Make all changes on the worksheet.

EXAMPLE Katie likes to bake more than ~~dancing~~ she likes to dance.

______ **1.** Ricardo's favorite activities are yearbook staff, chess club, and taking violin lessons.

______ **2.** This school provides more classes for students interested in science than art.

______ **3.** Colleges look at applicants' grades and what their extracurricular activities are.

______ **4.** Waving wildly and with loud cheers, the crowd celebrated the winning goal.

______ **5.** The radio announced that traffic was unusually heavy because of three collisions, construction on the bridge, and the weather was bad.

______ **6.** We ride the bus to school in the morning, and walking is how we get home in the afternoon.

______ **7.** Having a part-time job is rewarding, but it takes a lot of responsibility, energy, and time.

______ **8.** To have her own car, Tamara needs to pay half of the insurance, buy her own gas, and a B grade average.

______ **9.** I will go to drama camp during July and August after returning from a visit with my grandparents.

______ **10.** Learning from your successes is easy, but to learn from your mistakes is not.

______ **11.** Asking for help is almost always better than to fail.

______ **12.** The students requested more extracurricular options and to have a study hall period.

Revising Stringy Sentences

DIRECTIONS Decide which of the following sentences are stringy and need revision. Revise the sentences in these ways:

- Break the sentence into two or more sentences.
- Turn an independent clause into a subordinate clause.
- Turn an independent clause into a phrase.
- If a sentence needs no revision, write C.
- Make all changes on the worksheet.

EXAMPLE Lizards, ~~are reptiles, and they are~~ the biggest living group of reptiles, ~~and they~~ belong to the order that includes snakes. ~~and~~ There are more than 3,000 species of lizards.

_____ **1.** Lizards are interesting, often colorful creatures that live in most parts of the world, although few species are found in the higher latitudes.

_____ **2.** Most types of lizards live in tropical and subtropical areas of the world, and a few types are found in temperate regions, and none live in arctic regions.

_____ **3.** Some lizards live in burrows, and some live in trees, and some live part of the time in water, but iguanas live in all three habitats.

_____ **4.** Lizards and snakes are similar, but there are also differences, and the differences are that most lizards have legs and that the lower jaw of most lizards is in one piece.

_____ **5.** Lizards are ectothermic, which means they are coldblooded and tend to take on the temperature of their surroundings.

_____ **6.** Lizards are similar in appearance to salamanders, but most lizards have clawed feet and external ear openings, and salamanders do not have these features.

_____ **7.** Most lizards are harmless and help people by eating insects, and some lizards are a source of food.

_____ **8.** Lizards eat many different things, and most of them eat insects, but the green iguana eats plants, and the Gila monster eats eggs and small rodents.

Revising Stringy Sentences

DIRECTIONS Decide which of the following sentences are stringy and need revision. Revise the sentences in these ways:

- Break the sentence into two or more sentences.
- Turn an independent clause into a subordinate clause.
- Turn an independent clause into a phrase.
- If a sentence needs no revision, write C.
- Make all changes on the worksheet.

EXAMPLE Although Many people have seen cartoons or animated movies, ~~but~~ they might not realize how animation works. ~~and~~ It is not a simple process.

_____ **1.** Animation creates the illusion of movement, but it is actually a series of still images or objects, and they are shown in rapid succession.

_____ **2.** Because movie film runs at 24 frames per second, an animator must create 72 images for an action that takes a character only 3 seconds.

_____ **3.** Early animated films ran in movie theaters along with feature films, and they were called cartoons, and the cartoons were less than ten minutes long.

_____ **4.** Longer animated films are often based on fantasy, and they are often based on historical subjects.

_____ **5.** Walt Disney was a pioneer in the art of animation, and he created Mickey Mouse, and Mickey Mouse is the most famous animated character in history.

_____ **6.** Pinscreen animation was developed in France, and it uses millions of pins sticking through a large upright frame, and rollers push the pins either in or out, and the pins' shadows are filmed.

_____ **7.** Pixilation is another type of animation, and people are posed and moved short distances, but the effect is of very strange movement, and this effect occurs when the film is played.

_____ **8.** Puppet animation and clay animation are special kinds of animation, and the animator moves three-dimensional figures very slightly for each frame of film, and the illusion of movement is achieved.

Revising Wordy Sentences

DIRECTIONS Revise the following paragraph, eliminating wordiness to make it clearer and more effective.

- Eliminate wordiness.
- Add details if you wish.

When they think of the phenomenon of hypnotism, most people imagine and picture a stage show or a television show that stars or features a flamboyant entertainer who invites and brings volunteer people up onto the stage to perform a series of different hilarious actions. But actually, in reality, the practice of hypnotism has been widely and generally accepted by the participants and members of groups such as medical, dental, and psychological associations around the world. Nobody seems to know for sure exactly how hypnotism actually works, but it seems to be based on the idea that there is a thing called suggestibility. Subjects, to begin with, are first put into a state or condition of deep and complete total relaxation, and then the hypnotist who is performing the hypnosis gives them certain different suggestions. Results indicate that all of those subjects who respond appropriately and in a fitting way to these suggestions are highly suggestible and may even be helped to avoid bad habits, overcome fears, remember past events, and so on and so forth.

Revising Wordy Sentences

DIRECTIONS On a separate sheet of paper, revise the following paragraphs to make them clearer and more effective.

- Eliminate wordiness.
- Add details if you wish.

1. Mary Cassatt was a famous American impressionist painter who was born in the year 1844 and died in the year 1926. She is considered by many art experts and other people to be one of the group of a number of painters who are known as the impressionists. She went to school and studied at the Pennsylvania Academy of the Fine Arts in Philadelphia, Pennsylvania, during the years of 1861 to 1866. Then she left the Pennsylvania Academy of the Fine Arts and went to Europe and eventually settled in Paris, France, to reside and paint. There she made the acquaintance of the French painter Edgar Degas. He saw her work, he liked it, and he thought it was very good. He invited her to join the other impressionist painters and exhibit her paintings along with paintings that they had done.

2. Arlene waited for her plane at the airport. She thought about and remembered the last trip that she had taken as a traveler, when she had carried a heavy three-pound cut of Limburger cheese in her flight bag on board the plane. The weighty three-pound cheese was a special gift to give to her grandparents. Arlene had been sure beyond the shadow of a doubt the cheese would stay fresh throughout the flight, but, unfortunately, the plane circumnavigated around the airport for several hours, and then it landed on the runway. Some of the passengers spent time trying to locate the source of a strange odor, but they couldn't find it. Arlene was embarrassed. She didn't want anyone to know she was the person who had brought the strong-smelling cheese aboard the plane, so she left the cheese on the plane. Although she left the cheese, she had a story to tell her grandparents and they found it quite amusing.

NAME CLASS DATE

for **CHAPTER 19: EXERCISE 10** page 502 **PRACTICE A, WORKSHEET 35**

Varying Sentence Beginnings

DIRECTIONS Revise the following sentences by varying their beginnings.

- Use the notes in parentheses to determine whether the sentence should start with a single-word modifier, a phrase, or a subordinate clause.
- Add or delete words as necessary to make the sentence sound better.

1. The public was highly entertained by silent films in the early days of moviemaking. (phrase)

2. Throngs of eager viewers filled movie theaters every Saturday. (phrase)

3. They laughed, cried, and applauded just as audiences do today. (subordinate clause)

4. Someone usually played a piano in the theater to accompany the action in the film. (single-word modifier)

5. Live actors or a narrator sometimes spoke from behind the screen to add interest. (phrase)

6. The stars of these first films had to be very expressive in their use of gestures because there was no dialogue. (subordinate clause)

7. Moviemakers congregated in Hollywood, California, and developed a film community. (phrase)

8. Some of them were experts at cinematic storytelling and made as many as two films a week. (phrase)

9. Silent films began to be replaced by "talkies" in the late 1920s. (phrase)

10. It may seem surprising, but many of the silent movie stars are still sentimental favorites. (subordinate clause)

Varying Sentence Beginnings

DIRECTIONS Revise the following sentences by varying their beginnings.

- Use the notes in parentheses to determine whether the sentence should start with a single-word modifier, a phrase, or a subordinate clause.
- Add or delete words as necessary to make the sentence sound better.

1. Humans have had a special relationship with dogs for thousands of years. (phrase)

2. Humans bonded with wolves originally. (single-word modifier)

3. Humans and wolves got along well together because they both live in groups. (subordinate clause)

4. Wolves began to treat humans as leaders of their pack when they saw that humans were better hunters than they were. (subordinate clause)

5. Humans probably began to adopt wolf cubs over time. (phrase)

6. These wolves were willing to obey humans and became helpful hunting partners. (phrase)

7. Humans and early dogs probably made good companions since they shared an interest in hunting. (subordinate clause)

8. The first figure of a dog appears around 4500 B.C. in a cave painting of a hunting scene. (phrase)

9. The dog in the painting, a helpful companion, probably played the same role that dogs do today. (phrase)

10. Most dogs want to be wherever their owners are. (subordinate clause)

Revising Sentences to Create Variety

DIRECTIONS Each of the sentences in the following paragraph begins with a subject. Underline a word or group of words that could be placed at the beginning of the sentence.

1. My brother has more fear than fun in the woods. He is always on the lookout for poison ivy because he is allergic to it. He also worries about snakes and spiders. He is fearful and tiptoes through the woods, scanning the underbrush. He walks very quickly most of the time. He misses the best part of the great outdoors because he is worried about all these things. He pays attention only to the sticks and dead leaves beneath his feet and ignores the colors, movement, and sounds of the woods.

DIRECTIONS Use what you have learned about varying sentence beginnings to revise the following paragraph. Reword some sentences so that they begin with phrases, clauses, or single-word modifiers. Some sentences may be reworded in several ways; choose the way that seems best. (Consult the chart on page 501 of your textbook for help.)

2. It isn't very pleasant to walk in a heavy downpour. My sister and I recently found this out for ourselves. We left a basketball game at school one afternoon just as it began to rain. My sister's car ran out of gas on the way home. We trudged through the downpour to the nearest gas station. We returned to the car after we filled the gas can. We were both wet and grumpy, and we argued all the way home.

Revising Sentences to Create Variety

DIRECTIONS Each of the sentences in the following paragraph begins with a subject. Underline a word or group of words that could be placed at the beginning of the sentence.

1. Tarzan is a fictional character who was created by writer Edgar Rice Burroughs. So many people have read stories and seen movies about Tarzan that he has taken on a kind of reality in spite of his fictional nature. Tarzan's parents died in Africa when he was young. This mythical hero was fortunate to be found and raised by apes. He then went on to have adventures all over the world. Tarzan became, in time, one of the most famous people who never was.

DIRECTIONS Use what you have learned about varying sentence beginnings to revise the following paragraph. Reword some sentences so that they begin with phrases, clauses, or single-word modifiers. Some sentences may be reworded in several ways; choose the way that seems best. (Consult the chart on page 501 of your textbook for help.)

2. Christo is a "wrap artist" who was born in Bulgaria in 1935. He received formal training but rebelled against the rules of art and began to create very unusual works. He put up 1,760 huge yellow umbrellas in Tejon Pass north of Los Angeles. He used sixty-two pieces of brown tarpaulin and two miles of rope to wrap the Museum of Contemporary Art in Chicago. He hung an orange curtain between two mountains in Rifle, Colorado. Christo does not earn money from these projects because they are enormous and public. He finances his work, instead, by selling sketches and models of his projects.

Revising a Paragraph

DIRECTIONS The following paragraphs have many of the problems reviewed in this section. On a separate sheet of paper, rewrite and revise the paragraphs to improve style.

- Correct nonparallel structure.
- Correct stringy and wordy sentences.
- Vary sentence beginnings, and add or delete details as necessary.

1. Some people have the wrong idea about the dogs called poodles, and these people don't know much about the poodle breed. They think poodles are fancy, and they also think these dogs are useless and not good for anything, but this is far from true. Poodles were originally developed as a sporting breed. Poodles are used as retrievers, by police departments, and as Seeing Eye dogs. Poodles are smart and learn tricks very quickly, and so they also are used as performers in plays and circuses. Poodles are classified by three basic sizes. The basic sizes are standard, miniature, and toy.

2. People have been concerned about dental hygiene and keeping their teeth clean for hundreds and thousands of years. The Egyptians are one early example, for instance. They used a "chew stick," and it was about the size of a pencil. This utensil was frayed at one end, being soft and brushlike. In China, later, people plucked bristles from the backs of the necks of hogs and attached them to handles made of bamboo, or they fastened them to handles made of bone. Hog bristles were too stiff for comfort for Europeans, and their preference was toothbrushes fabricated of horsehair, but new materials were necessitated because damp bristles cut the skin of the mouth and caused infections as one of the results. A toothbrush with gentle nylon bristles was sold in 1938, and it dried more easily between brushings, and this prevented bacterial growth.

Revising a Paragraph

DIRECTIONS The following paragraphs have many of the problems reviewed in this section. Rewrite and revise the paragraphs to improve style.

- Correct nonparallel structure.
- Correct stringy and wordy sentences.
- Vary sentence beginnings, and add or delete details as necessary.

1. The Siamese is a pedigreed cat, and most people recognize a Siamese cat instantly. It is noted for its beautiful coat and that it has deep-blue eyes. It is a medium-sized feline. It has a long body, and it has a thin tail, and having a wedge-shaped head. Siamese kittens are born white or nearly so and later develop the characteristic darker colors on the face, ears, paws, and tail, and these parts of the cat are called points. One more thing is that the Siamese is highly intelligent. Its cries are loud and complaining, and it easily communicates about its needs to the person who owns it. The cat really "owns" the owner in effect.

2. There are thousands of species of snails. They live in marine environments. They live in freshwater environments, and live on land, too. Snails are termed "gastropods," and this means "belly-footed," and they mostly feed on mainly algae and decaying matter, and the snail has numerous "denticles," or teeth, and they protrude and stick out from the snail's ribbonlike tongue that looks a lot like a ribbon unfurling. The eyes of many species are located on the tentacles. Snails have an unusual method of movement that is interesting, and they do that by contracting muscles in their organ of locomotion, and that is called the foot.

Identifying Main Ideas and Topic Sentences

DIRECTIONS Each of the following paragraphs develops a main idea.

- If there is a topic sentence, underline it. If there is no topic sentence, look for the main idea in the details of the paragraph.
- State the main idea of each paragraph.

1. The Hindu calendar is different from the solar calendar used in Western cultures. The Hindu calendar is a lunar calendar, based on cycles of the moon. The calendar is made up of about 354 days, divided into twelve months. A thirteenth month is added every thirty months to align the lunar calendar with the solar calendar. The days of the Hindu month are named for sections of the sky called *nakshatra*.

Main idea: ______________________________

____

2. When the Cherokee lived in what is now the southeastern United States, their houses were simple and made from materials that could be found nearby. The houses were built of hickory, pine, or cedar logs. Roofs were made of bark. There was a smoke hole in the roof.

Main idea: ______________________________

____

3. In the spring, the people of China celebrate a festival called Ching Ming. Ching Ming usually falls in what Western cultures know as the month of April. During this time, Chinese people visit the graves of their ancestors. They clear weeds from the grave sites and make offerings to the departed. Ching Ming gives Chinese people an opportunity to acknowledge the importance of those who have come before them.

Main idea: ______________________________

____

4. It is February 2, Groundhog Day. Every year on this day, a groundhog in Pennsylvania supposedly climbs out of its hole and tries to see its shadow. If the groundhog sees its shadow, winter will last six more weeks. If the day is cloudy and the groundhog can't see its shadow, spring weather will arrive soon.

Main idea: ______________________________

____

Collecting Supporting Details

DIRECTIONS Four general ideas you could write about are listed below. With each idea, a type of support—examples, facts and statistics, or sensory details—is suggested.

- Think of two details to support each main idea, and write them in the chart below.
- You may have to do some research (reading or talking to knowledgeable people) to find support, especially facts or statistics.

MAIN IDEA	SUPPORT
1. Many women have fought for human rights.	Examples
2. Puffins are fascinating sea birds.	Facts and Statistics
3. After exercising, the first thing people often want is a glass of cold water.	Sensory Details
4. On the Fourth of July, the people of the United States celebrate the nation's independence.	Examples

Writing a Clincher Sentence

DIRECTIONS The paragraphs below do not have clincher sentences.

- Read each paragraph and determine what its main idea is.
- Then, for each paragraph, write a clincher sentence that (1) emphasizes the main idea and (2) signals that the end of the paragraph has come. (Try to include a transitional word or phrase.)

1. Although the woods are beautiful, hazards lurk there. Watch for insects that bite or sting. Be careful to avoid poison ivy and poison oak, and do not eat any berry you cannot identify.

Clincher sentence: ____________________

2. Taking good photographs requires some planning. Consider whether most of the pictures will be taken indoors or outdoors and whether you will be using a flash. For each picture, consider how close to your subject you want to be.

Clincher sentence: ____________________

3. The Huntington Botanical Gardens in San Marino, California, not far from downtown Los Angeles, is a remarkable place. Its assortment of plants and flowers includes specimens from all over the world. You can see everything from lotus blossoms to exotic cacti. A library containing rare books and manuscripts and galleries displaying famous paintings are located on the same grounds.

Clincher sentence: ____________________

4. The hues of autumn are everywhere. From my window I can see the vivid red of Mr. Woo's maple tree. Across the street is the bright yellow of the Paxton family's chestnut tree. Down the street I can see the deep burgundy of the Skowroneks' ash tree.

Clincher sentence: ____________________

Identifying Sentences That Destroy Unity

DIRECTIONS Draw a line through the sentences that destroy unity in the following paragraphs. Remember: To have unity, all details in a paragraph must be related to the topic sentence (main idea) or the sequence of actions.

1. Modeling is usually presented as a glamorous career, but in reality it has some drawbacks. The hours are long, often beginning early in the morning. The taller you are, the more likely it is that you'll be able to be a model. Because models work with different photographers at different studios every day, they often find it difficult to make and keep friendships with people with whom they work. Although models wear beautiful clothes in front of the camera, they almost never get to keep them.

2. The composer and band leader Duke Ellington had a long and very sucessful career as a jazz musician. Born in 1899, Ellington began studying piano when he was seven and started playing professionally at age seventeen. His father enjoyed music as well. Between 1928 and 1931, Ellington recorded 160 albums. Ellington and his band also appeared in several movies during the 1930s. During his lifetime, Ellington composed numerous songs, sacred music, and longer works, including film scores and a ballet. Ellington died in 1974.

3. The first step in doing laundry is to sort the clothes. Clothes that are very dark or very bright can tint white or light-colored clothes if they are washed together. Therefore, you should separate white clothes from colored ones. Also, separate clothes you plan to bleach from those that should not be bleached. You can save money by clipping coupons for bleach and laundry detergent. Be sure to set aside heavily soiled clothes for pre-soaking. Finally, do not wash clothes that produce lint, such as towels, with clothes that attract lint, such as corduroy pants.

4. American society is becoming more mobile, with about three out of ten families moving each year. Many move because a family member is looking for a job. Some move because a family member has been transferred to a new job. Other families move simply because they prefer a different location. Some family members may not be happy about moving to a new residence.

Choosing an Order of Ideas

DIRECTIONS Indicate which order (chronological order, spatial order, order of importance, or logical order) would work best for explaining each of the following topics. For some topics, you may indicate that more than one type of order would work well. Briefly explain your choices.

1. taking care of puppies ____________________

2. choosing a good doctor ____________________

3. the rules of a game ____________________

4. driving to a vacation spot ____________________

5. writing a research paper ____________________

6. a recipe for baking bread ____________________

7. the layout of your school ____________________

8. four characteristics of a friend ____________________

9. the best and the worst summer vacations ____________________

10. why a short story is excellent ____________________

11. writing a poem ____________________

12. three characteristics of a great television program ____________________

Identifying Direct References and Transitions

DIRECTIONS The following paragraphs use both direct references and transitional words and phrases to connect ideas. For each paragraph, make two lists in the space provided: one list of direct reference words and one list of transitions you find in the paragraph.

1. In December 1955, Rosa Parks was arrested when she deliberately broke the segregation laws of Montgomery, Alabama, by refusing to leave a seat reserved for whites in the front section of a city bus. As a result, many African Americans in Montgomery boycotted the city buses to protest the seating laws. The boycott was a hardship because some had no other way to reach work or other places. Because of her action, Parks received threatening phone calls and was fired from her job. Her husband also lost his job. Despite the difficulties experienced by so many people, the bus boycott continued in Montgomery for 381 days, until the Supreme Court ruled that racial segregation on city buses was unconstitutional.

Direct References	Transitions

2. Characterized as brave and loyal in the long-running television series *Lassie*, the collie ranks as one of the most popular of more than 125 dog breeds recognized by the American Kennel Club. Of the two types of collies, the rough-coated Lassie type is far more popular than the smooth-coated collie. Both types were developed in Scotland from a black-and-white sheepdog. Today, collies come in four main color patterns, the most common one being sable and white. Sable refers to colors ranging from gold to dark brown. A white blaze often adorns the collie's face. All types of collies have long beautiful coats, with feathering behind the legs.

Direct References	Transitions

NAME CLASS DATE

for **CHAPTER 20: EXERCISE 7** page 525 **WORKSHEET 47**

Using Transitions

DIRECTIONS The following passages are not completely clear. Revise each passage by adding transitions to make the connections it needs. Feel free to rewrite or combine sentences, too. Mark your changes in the text of the passage.

1. I really wanted a job working outdoors with children for the summer. I heard that the city recreation department was looking for day camp counselors. I went to City Hall to get an application. There were a lot of other people my age waiting in line. I did not become discouraged. I filled out the application and handed it in. I waited. I received a call from the recreation department. I had experience taking care of my younger nieces and nephews during the summer. The head of the department was interested in interviewing me.

2. If orange carrots bore you, consider trying a new maroon-skinned carrot (still orange on the inside). Maroon carrots are extra crunchy and sweet. They have double the usual amount of beta carotene. The extra beta carotene is a plus. Beta carotene helps prevent cancer and heart disease. Researchers at the Vegetable Improvement Center, part of Texas A & M University, developed the BetaSweet carrot. They thought the carrot would provide some fun and boost school spirit. The university's colors are white and maroon. BetaSweet carrots were marketed in packages designed to attract children. The packages show cartoon characters of a family called the Beta Bunch.

Elaborating with Details

DIRECTIONS The following paragraphs lack elaboration. Add sensory details, examples, or facts and statistics to develop or expand on the ideas already present in each paragraph. To find facts and statistics, you will need to do some research. To find other details, you may want to work with a partner.

1. A good stage actor needs certain qualities. The actor must be able to remember the lines. Actors need good imaginations. A flexible body and the ability to move well are usually important. The performer needs the ability to cooperate and be part of a team. These are the qualities of a good stage actor.

2. In the past, veterinarians principally focused on the cure and treatment of disease in animals. Now they pay close attention to other aspects of animal health as well. As a result of changes in the field, veterinary schools have improved their programs. The schools offer new courses and require students to attend school for longer periods of time.

Dividing a Passage into Paragraphs

DIRECTIONS The passage that follows was originally broken into three paragraphs.

- Indicate where you think the paragraph breaks went—or should go.
- Then, on the lines provided, explain your choices.

Biologists are increasingly excited about a technique called phytoremediation. The word is from the Greek words *phyto,* meaning "plant" and *remediate,* meaning "to repair." It is the process of using plants to remove pollutants from soil, water, and air. Several plants, such as Indian mustard, poplar trees, and sunflowers, have taken in toxic metals without harm to their growth. After absorbing the toxic waste, the plants can be harvested and burned to recover valuable absorbed metals, such as copper and nickel. One plant being used successfully in this process is the yellow poplar tree. This tree can grow up to fifteen feet a year and absorb twenty-five gallons of liquid a day. Its large root system acts as a giant straw, absorbing crude oil, metals, pesticides, and/or solvents. The tree breaks down the harmful materials, releasing some of the byproducts in less toxic forms through its leaves. Although using this process to clean up a site may take several years, it is less expensive than other methods. On-site soil cleanup can cost between $10 and $100 per cubic meter. Using plants would cost about five cents per cubic meter. In addition, the plants beautify the site. Sites being targeted for this method include streams, abandoned mines, oil spills, and city waste heaps.

Explanation for Paragraph Breaks:

Section 3: More Practice with Combining Sentences

Combining Notes into Sentences

By making notes, you can generate a lot of ideas very quickly without stopping to decide how, where, or even if you will eventually use them. Notes need not follow any specific logical order. In fact, they are usually composed of words, phrases, and clauses instead of complete sentences. Making notes is a great way to begin writing. However, when it comes time to begin the first draft, you must turn your notes into sentences.

Writer's Notes: tenth-grade classes
fixing up an old playground
children who live in the neighborhood
over the past year

Sentence: Over the past year, the tenth-grade classes have been fixing up an old playground for the neighborhood children.

Remember that a **sentence** is a group of words that contains a subject and a verb and expresses a complete thought. Make sure that each of your sentences meets each of these qualifications.

DIRECTIONS Combine the following notes to form complete sentences. Insert punctuation and capitalization when necessary.

1. the playground has been neglected
   quiet, sleepy neighborhood
   no children have used it
   for several years

2. swing set is rusty
   near the large oak
   looks as though a truck ran into it
   tilting at an impossible angle

3. the baseball diamond
   not used in decades
   grown over with tall, prickly weeds
   west side of park

4. small birds
   have staked their claim
   building nests for young
   behind home plate
   underneath the bleachers

5. the sandbox
a few wild flowers
play with my trucks
used to be favorite place
now filled with weeds

6. at a town meeting
get new playground equipment
suggested we clean up the park
a group of high school students

7. eager to help
volunteered to work
baseball diamond
ready to see a change
my father and I

8. interest in a new playground
happy to encourage students
many enthusiastic people
offered their time and skills

9. using our free time
mowing
pulling weeds
building up the pitcher's mound
worked whenever we could

10. on a warm, balmy day
imagining the smack of a bat
I worked quickly
leveling the dirt
for the new home plate

Using Compound Elements

"Birds of a feather flock together." In writing, that observation becomes advice. Good writers keep similar elements together.

When you read over your first draft, you may notice two or more sentences that are quite similar. Perhaps only the subject, the verb, or the complement is different. These types of sentences can easily be combined by using coordinating conjunctions.

Coordinating Conjunctions

and but or nor for so yet

Original: Janet raises dogs. Her sister does, too.
Combined: Janet *and* her sister raise dogs.
(Here the subjects have been combined.)

Original: Does Janet's brother also raise dogs? Does he train them?
Combined: Does Janet's brother also raise *or* train dogs?
(Here the verbs have been combined.)

Original: Janet's dogs are big. They are very gentle.
Combined: Janet's dogs are big *yet* very gentle.
(Here the complements have been combined.)

NOTE: Remember to use commas to separate items in a series.
Janet raises, trains, and shows Irish wolfhounds.

You can also use a coordinating conjunction to join whole sentences. The conjunction you choose depends on the meaning you want the sentence to have. One little word can make a *big* difference in meaning.

Original: Janet likes dogs. Her sister likes cats.
Combined: Janet likes dogs, *and* her sister likes cats.
Janet likes dogs, *yet* her sister likes cats.
Janet likes dogs, *but* her sister likes cats.
Janet likes dogs, *so* her sister likes cats.
Janet likes dogs, *for* her sister likes cats.

When you read over your draft, look for places where words are repeated. These may be places for compound elements.

DIRECTIONS Join the compound elements in the following sets of sentences. Add commas when necessary.

- Change, add, or delete words to make the new sentences read correctly.
- Make your changes on the worksheet.

EXAMPLE We laughed until we cried, ~~At same time~~ yet we felt horrified.

1. Emilio outlined his ideas for the advertising campaign. He got his client's approval.
2. The topics Mr. Gorush suggested for our persuasive essays were capital punishment gun control and mandatory military service. None of them appealed to me.
3. A typical meal at Graziella's is delicious. It is far too large for only one person.
4. Sophie has an athletic scholarship to a college in upper Michigan. Her brother has one, too.
5. I was proud of the pair of men's pajamas I made for Life Skills class. My brother's reaction to them was typical.
6. Last night my cousin Connie suggested that we volunteer at the children's hospital. Her mom, who is a nurse, also suggested it.
7. Phil's dog, Sparky, has never had any training. He barks all night, sleeps on the sofa, and takes food right off your plate.
8. Ms. Groton, who called Andy into her office for another discussion about athletics vs. algebra, was happy that Andy's grades improved. She was sure that he could do even better.
9. A career in marine biology is important to Elaine. She is taking additional science courses this summer.
10. My plan for a dog food commercial is based on three themes: the Seven Wonders of the World the lunar landing and life in the future. My plan may also be used for a birdseed commercial.

Using Semicolons

When you write a first draft, ideas often come just one at a time. Consequently, your first draft may have many short sentences. However, when you read your draft over, you will realize that some of these sentences are related to each other. When you find these pairs of sentences, you'll need to connect them. There are many ways to connect sentences Semicolons are one of these ways.

When you decide to use a semicolon to connect sentences, make sure that the sentences are very closely related and equally important.

Related Sentences: Our drama department is quite active. It produces three plays each year.

Combined: Our drama department is quite active; it produces three plays each year.

Sentences that are not closely related should *not* be combined.

Unrelated Sentences: I had never auditioned before. The competition was surprisingly fierce.

As you learn to use semicolons to connect related sentences, you will find that you will be able to express complicated thoughts easily. Consequently, your writing will be far more likely to impress your readers; you may even impress yourself.

DIRECTIONS Decide whether each pair of sentences should be combined. Make your changes on the worksheet.

- If a pair should be combined, replace the period with a semicolon.
- If a pair should not be combined, circle the period.

EXAMPLES The audience was wildly enthusiastic; They didn't even seem to notice when we flubbed our lines.

Our costumes were not backstage. We hadn't expected to perform in ordinary clothes.

1. When I started high school, I knew I wanted to join the drama department. Performing on stage was a dream of mine.

2. Besides taking classes in theater, I would be auditioning for roles. As a child, I was very self-conscious.

3. Upperclassmen usually got the leading roles. Freshmen and sophomores had to pay their dues by working as stagehands.

4. I remember the first play of the season—*A Midsummer Night's Dream*. It has always been one of my favorites.

5. Playing Puck would be a dream come true. I studied the role until I had memorized every line, right down to the stage directions.

6. I knew it was a long shot, but I tried out for the role. The microphone was at exactly the wrong angle.

7. As an understudy, you must learn the lines as though you actually had the role. It was an easy job for me.

8. When opening night was a week away, there was no indication that I would be needed. Our Puck, Tad MacIntyre, was as healthy as an aerobics instructor.

9. Suddenly, it happened. Tad got laryngitis the night before we opened.

10. I had the opportunity I had dreamed about. Tad recovered quickly and was back onstage after three nights.

Using Colons, Dashes, and Parentheses

Punctuation marks are usually thought of as ways to *separate* ideas. However, some punctuation marks can be used to *join* facts, ideas, and other types of information. You can even use these punctuation marks to combine sentences. **Colons, dashes,** and **parentheses** are three of these types of marks.

When one sentence merely names a series of items, consider using a colon to connect the series to another sentence.

Original: I used several types of materials for my handmade brochure. They were *paper, colored pens, glue, and pictures.*

Combined: I used the following materials for my handmade brochure: *paper, colored pens, glue, and pictures.*

Using a colon to combine sentences can help you make a dramatic statement.

Original: I was certain of only one thing. I wanted it to look professional.

Combined: I was certain of only one thing: I wanted it to look professional.

Dashes and parentheses can add variety to your writing. They can help vary your tone, changing your voice or that of a character.

A dash can allow you to insert a whole idea, even a whole sentence, right into the middle of another sentence.

Original: My photograph showed a sandy beach and palm trees. *It was the most perfect beach in the world!*

Combined: My photograph showed a sandy beach—*the most perfect beach in the world!*—and palm trees.

A dash can also mean *namely, that is,* or *in other words.*

Original: Visitors come to the island mainly for three reasons. *They want to relax, fish, and swim.*

Combined: Visitors come to the island mainly for three reasons—*relaxing, fishing, and swimming.*

With parentheses, you can include interesting information that might not be of major importance.

Original: Actually, my mother gave me some ideas. *She's a travel agent.*

Combined: Actually, my mother (*she's a travel agent*) gave me some ideas.

DIRECTIONS Combine each of the sets of sentences on the next page into a single sentence.

- For the first four sentences, combine the sentences by using the mark of punctuation that appears in italics at the end of the item.
- For the last four sentences, choose whatever mark of punctuation you think is appropriate—a colon, a dash(es) or parentheses.

1. My travel brochure was due on November 11. It had to be complete, not a rough draft. (*paired dashes*)

2. My brochure was intended to entice travelers to an imaginary tropical island. The brochure was a lovely three-page spread. (*parens*)

3. Flights depart for this island three days a week. The days are Tuesday, Thursday, and Friday. (*colon*)

4. Travelers would want to visit this island for several reasons. There are pristine beaches, friendly people, tropical plants, and delicious food. (*dash*)

5. The island features another spectacular attraction. It has an active volcano.

6. If you take the weekend special, you can save quite a bit of money. By the way, it is not advertised.

7. When I prepared my brochure, I made sure to use descriptive terms and tantalizing photos. It was the best in the class.

8. I chose to highlight three main ideas. These were the daytime activities, the quality of the accommodations, and the island's beauty.

Using Correlative Conjunctions

Some things just go together—right and left, hammer and nails, or rock and roll, for instance. One half of the pair isn't much good without the other. Each one of the pair needs the other to function. **Correlative conjunctions** are connecting words that come in pairs. When you use one, you usually use the other.

Correlative Conjunctions

both . . . and	not only . . . but also	either . . . or
neither . . . nor	whether . . . or	

You can use correlative conjunctions to show relationships between ideas of equal importance. Use *not only . . . but also* or *both . . . and* to indicate an additional important idea.

Original: We did a lot of sightseeing. We visited our relatives as well.

Combined: *Not only* did we do a lot of sightseeing, but we also visited our relatives.

Use *either . . . or, neither . . . nor,* or *whether . . . or* to indicate a choice between alternatives.

Original: We tried to decide. We could buy shoes or a jacket to take home.

Combined: We tried to decide *whether* to buy shoes *or* a jacket to take home.

Keep in mind that you may need to change a word or two when you use correlative conjunctions to combine sentences. Be sure to read your revision over carefully so that you can smooth out any bumps.

DIRECTIONS Use correlative conjunctions to combine the following sets of sentences.

- For the first five items, use the correlative conjunctions in parentheses.
- For the second five items, use the correlative conjunctions that best fit the meaning of the sentences.

EXAMPLE My cousin and I visited our relatives in Italy last summer. We toured some of Italy's most famous cities. (*not only . . . but also*)

My cousin and I not only visited our relatives in Italy last summer, but we also toured some of Italy's most famous cities.

1. Our trip to Italy introduced us to a beautiful country. It allowed us to see some magnificent art. (*not only . . . but also*)

2. We stayed at the homes of relatives. We found inexpensive hotels that catered to students. *(either . . . or)*

3. Our inability to speak Italian fluently did not discourage us. Our inexperience with foreign travel didn't discourage us. *(neither . . . nor)*

4. Because our time was limited, we had to decide. We could spend a few hours or a few days in each city. *(whether . . . or)*

5. While we were in Rome, we visited the Colosseum. We also visited the Vatican Museum. *(both . . . and)*

6. We went to St. Peter's Basilica. We climbed to the top of the dome.

7. In Florence, we spent our time in museums. We window-shopped and drank hot chocolate at outdoor cafes.

8. The road from Florence to Pisa is short. It is also scenic.

9. The famous Leaning Tower of Pisa does lean. It is also in real danger of collapsing.

10. At the end of our stay, we had to decide. We could fly home with a stop in Paris, or we could travel by train through Europe and leave from Brussels.

Combining and Varying Sentences I

If you ate your favorite kind of sandwich for lunch every day, you'd probably tire of it rapidly. No matter how good something tastes or how much you like it, you want some variety. The same principle applies to writing. If your writing style never varies, it quickly becomes boring. You can make sure that your writing is always fresh and interesting by varying sentence structure.

The most common beginning for a sentence is a subject followed by a verb.

Monica left for the trip with a twenty-pound backpack and her cocker spaniel.

The Homecoming dance was scheduled for October 16.

This word order is clear and precise, but constant repetition of the subject-verb pattern is too much of a good thing. Adding introductory words, phrases, and clauses to sentence beginnings will keep your writing style varied and engaging.

Basic: Joe took matters into his own hands imperturbably.
Varied: *Imperturbably*, Joe took matters into his own hands.

Basic: We saw the remains of a chicken coop in the backyard of the old house.
Varied: *In the backyard of the old house*, we saw the remains of a chicken coop.

Basic: The tennis team sponsored a picnic to welcome new members.
Varied: *To welcome new members*, the tennis team sponsored a picnic.

Basic: Our cat had to endure many baths after she challenged a skunk.
Varied: *After she challenged a skunk*, our cat had to endure many baths.

DIRECTIONS Combine each set of the following sentences in two different ways, varying the beginnings of sentences.

EXAMPLE It was the second time this week. The dog had eaten her homework. Marty was furious.

a. For the second time this week, the dog had eaten her homework, and Marty was furious.

b. Because the dog had eaten her homework for the second time this week, Marty was furious.

1. Hurricane Gabe struck the coast more ferociously than any storm in recent memory. The howling winds forced torrential rain through the streets.

   a. ______________________________

   ____

   b. ______________________________

   ____

2. The Emancipation Proclamation was issued during the Civil War. It did not end slavery. Slavery was banned throughout the United States only after the war.

a. ______________________________

____

b. ______________________________

____

3. The last game of the season was a terrible disappointment. It went to eleven innings before the Hornets won and saddened our supporters.

a. ______________________________

____

b. ______________________________

____

4. Colonists dumped tea into Boston Harbor. They were angry about a tea tax. This was only the beginning of a violent reaction against taxation without representation.

a. ______________________________

____

b. ______________________________

____

5. We finished tracing the computation error in our science experiment. It was much more difficult than we had thought it would be. We were exhausted.

a. ______________________________

____

b. ______________________________

____

Using Adjectives and Adverbs

When you read a book, you want to be able to imagine the events. If you are reading about a beach scene, you want to be able to *see* the gulls, *hear* the roar of the ocean, *taste* the salt water, *smell* the fresh air, and *feel* the grit of the sand.

Adjectives are the words that give this kind of information. An **adjective** is a word used to modify a noun or a pronoun.

Original: The boy wanted the toy robot. It was expensive. The boy was excited.

Combined: The *excited* boy wanted the *expensive* toy robot.

Not only do readers want to read specific descriptions of people, places, things, and ideas, but readers also want to know *how, when, where,* and *to what extent* the action is taking place.

Adverbs are the words that give this kind of information. An **adverb** is a word used to modify a verb, an adjective, or another adverb.

Original: The excited boy wanted the expensive toy robot. It was very expensive. He wanted it desperately.

Combined: The excited boy *desperately* wanted the *very* expensive toy robot.

NOTE: Remember to use commas to separate two or more modifiers preceding a noun.

DIRECTIONS Use adjectives and adverbs to combine the following sets of sentences. Decide whether you need to use commas or *and*.

EXAMPLE Before the hurricane, clouds scudded across the sky.

The clouds were steely gray. The clouds were moving rapidly.

Before the hurricane, steely gray clouds scudded rapidly across the sky.

1. Cecilia's swollen eyes were the result of a weekend with her sister's cat.

Her eyes were itchy. The cat was affectionate.
The cat was longhaired. The cat was a Persian.

2. After Julio studied for the math exam, he played some chords quietly on his uncle's guitar.

He studied diligently. He played quietly.

3. The counselor decided to recommend Alicia for advanced placement classes.

The counselor was intuitive. The counselor was confident.

4. When Grace was looking for her favorite purple socks, she disturbed several dust bunnies under her bed.

She looked frantically. The dust bunnies were enormous.

5. When I leaped the fence to get the basketball, the neighbors' beagle turned into fifteen pounds of fury.

The fury was snarling. The beagle was usually sweet-tempered.

6. After their performance, the band members congratulated one another and their surprised teacher.

The performance was award-winning. The band members were thrilled.
Their teacher's surprise was great.

7. Since Cleo forgot the road atlas, we were lost by the time we reached the bypass.

Cleo was absent-minded. The bypass was unfamiliar.
The bypass was congested. We reached the bypass finally.

8. When Moira opened the backpack, she was astonished to find a sandwich, a banana, her gym clothes, and a note from her algebra teacher.

The sandwich was half-eaten. The banana was black.
The gym clothes were unwashed. The note was old.
The note was unread.

Using Prepositional Phrases

Never hesitate to reduce the number of words, phrases, and sentences in your drafts. The more you concentrate your thoughts, the clearer they will be. You can use prepositional phrases to combine sentences and make your writing clearer, more interesting, and more powerful.

A **preposition** is a word that shows the relationship of a noun or a pronoun to some other word in the sentence.

Some Common Prepositions

about	at	for	over
according to	below	from	past
across	between	in front of	to
after	by	near	under
against	down	off	up
around	during	on	with

A **prepositional phrase** includes a preposition, a noun or a pronoun, and any modifiers of that noun or pronoun.

Original: Scott used his cell phone to call his office. He took the phone *from his briefcase*. He called *during a meeting*. His office is *in Chicago*.

Combined: *During a meeting,* Scott took his cell phone *from his briefcase* and used it to call his office *in Chicago*.

Notice that the phrase *to call his office* is not a prepositional phrase. Note, too, that *call* is not the object of a preposition. In addition to being a preposition, the word *to* also functions as the sign of an infinitive.

When you use prepositional phrases to combine sentences, take care to place phrases that modify nouns or pronouns as close as possible to the words they modify. Prepositional phrases that modify verbs, however, can appear anywhere in a sentence.

After the call on the cell phone, Scott hurriedly left the meeting.
Scott hurriedly left the meeting *after the call on the cell phone*.

DIRECTIONS For each of the following items, use prepositional phrases to create one sentence.

EXAMPLE Alexander Graham Bell founded a great company. His father-in-law helped him.

With help from his father-in-law, Alexander Graham Bell founded a great company.

1. The year of Alexander Graham Bell's birth was 1847. The place was Edinburgh, Scotland.

2. Bell immigrated. He went to Canada. He and his parents went there in 1870.

3. Bell established a school. It specialized in teaching people with impaired hearing. The school was in Boston, Massachusetts.

4. At the school, Bell performed many experiments. His experiments were with sound. They were with transmitting sound over wires.

5. Bell had a great dream. His dream was to help people whose hearing was impaired. His dream was to create a machine to help them.

6. Bell transmitted the first coherent spoken sentence. His assistant, Mr. Watson, received the message. The date was March 10, 1876.

7. Bell became a rich man. His invention made him rich. His invention was the telephone.

8. Bell helped other scientists. He used both his money and his interest in their work to do this.

9. Alexander Graham Bell died. The year was 1922. The place was his summer home, Nova Scotia, Canada.

10. At Bell's death, people paid their respects. They did not use the telephone.

Using Appositive Phrases

Sometimes you probably find that you are writing a sentence to explain something in a sentence you have already written. When this happens, you can often turn the sentence that explains into an appositive phrase.

An **appositive** is a noun or pronoun placed beside another noun or pronoun to identify or explain it. An **appositive phrase** is made up of an appositive and its modifiers.

Original: That ceramic bowl is inlaid with crystals. *It was a birthday gift.*
Combined: That ceramic bowl, *a birthday gift,* is inlaid with crystals.

NOTE: Appositive phrases are set off by commas.

With a little practice with appositive phrases, your writing will appear polished and you will sound knowledgeable.

DIRECTIONS Combine the following sentences. Use at least one appositive in each sentence. Punctuate and capitalize each sentence properly.

1. Pottery can be valuable or quite ordinary. Pottery consists of items made of baked clay.

2. Earthenware is a common type of pottery. It is covered by a colored glaze.

3. Stoneware is a heavy pottery fired at high temperatures. It can be glazed.

4. Two types of pottery are not usually glazed. These are a stoneware called jasper and an earthenware called terra cotta.

5. Fine china is soft-paste porcelain. Soft-paste porcelain is the most delicate type of pottery.

6. One of the oldest ways of making pottery is the coil method. It is also one of the simplest.

7. A potter's wheel is often electrically powered. It is one of the devices used to shape clay.

8. Kaolin is a fine, white clay. It is used in porcelain and is the reason fired porcelain has such delicate coloring.

Using Appositives to Begin Sentences

Have you ever found yourself sadly saying, "Well, I wish I had known that before"? By using appositive phrases at the beginning of a sentence, you can control when a reader learns certain facts and, thus, control your reader's reactions to your words.

An **appositive** is a noun or pronoun placed beside another noun or pronoun to identify or explain it. An **appositive phrase** is made up of an appositive and its modifiers.

Original: This poem focuses on a tree. *The poem is a masterpiece of symbolism.*
Combined: *A masterpiece of symbolism,* this poem focuses on a tree.

Notice that, in the original first sentence, the reader might be unimpressed by another poem about a tree. However, in the combined sentence, the reader is immediately aware that this poem is something special. The placement of the information in the appositive phrase has changed the reader's reaction.

Note: When you use an appositive phrase to begin a sentence, remember to use a comma at the end of the phrase.

DIRECTIONS Combine the following sets of sentences by using an appositive at the beginning of each sentence.

1. "Loveliest of Trees" appears in *A Shropshire Lad*, by A. E. Housman. It is a poem. The poem centers on a cherry tree in bloom.

2. The cherry tree is a symbol of spring. It also represents several other ideas.

3. The speaker reflects on how important it is to pay attention to beautiful things. The speaker is a young man.

4. The tree is described in a wistful manner. It is a metaphor for the brevity of life.

5. The speaker mentions *Eastertide*. The speaker is an appreciative observer of nature. *Eastertide* is a time for celebrating freshness and promise.

6. The speaker resolves to see as many "things in bloom" as he can. The speaker is one who knows that time and beauty pass quickly.

Using Participial Phrases

Action! That's the specialty of participles. When you read a sentence such as *The man was running*, your mind goes through a series of steps. First, you probably form a vague picture of a man. Then, you picture running. Last of all, you connect the words *man* and *running* and imagine a man running.

However, if you had read the expression *running man*, you would have seen a film in your mind, not a photograph. That film would have been rolling from the first word. Participles like *running* can turn a slide show into a movie.

A **participle** is a verb form that can be used as an adjective.

cut flowers, *painted* walls, *voting* booth, *broken* promises

A **participial phrase** consists of a participle and any complements or modifiers it may have. The entire participial phrase acts as an adjective.

You can create a participial phrase by taking the verb and its complements and modifiers out of one sentence and adding them to another sentence. Sometimes, you can even make this kind of revision without changing a word.

Original: People protested loudly. They were *tired of the overcrowding*.
Combined: People, *tired of the overcrowding*, protested loudly.
Combined: *Tired of the overcrowding*, people protested loudly.

At other times, you'll need to make small changes.

Original: Parents called the principal. *They had heard* about the proposal.
Combined: *Having heard* about the proposal, parents called the principal.

Because participles are verb forms, participial phrases can add life and action to your writing. When you use a participial phrase to combine sentences, you make your writing more exciting and more powerful.

DIRECTIONS Combine each set of sentences by inserting a participial phrase. The part to be inserted is underlined in the first five items. Set off participial phrases with commas.

EXAMPLE I <u>thought of my eighth-grade sister</u>. I decided to join the committee.
Thinking of my eighth-grade sister, I decided to join the committee.

1. The overcrowding at our school has created many problems. This was <u>caused by people moving to the suburbs</u>.

2. Frantic students trip over each other. They bump shoulders in the hallways. They try to get to class before the bell rings.

3. Some students avoid the busy hallways. They do not want to be late to class.

4. These dedicated students carry all their books. They are loaded down with heavy backpacks. They hope to avoid a stop at their lockers.

5. Many teachers frequently complain about the crowded halls. The teachers spend their free periods in their classrooms.

6. The principal decided to meet with the student council. He was frustrated by the situation.

7. The meeting was held in the school auditorium. It was called to propose possible solutions.

8. The student council suggested a longer time between classes. They exchanged ideas. They questioned other students.

9. Frustrated students proposed moving the lockers out of the crowded hallways. They insisted on more action.

10. Teachers suggested staggering class times. They wanted a quick solution to the problem.

Using Conjunctive Adverbs

You've been using conjunctive adverbs since you were about ten years old. Conjunctive adverbs are just ordinary words with a fancy name. When a conjunctive adverb joins two sentences, it shows a special relationship between the sentences. That relationship depends on the meaning of the adverb.

Conjunctive Adverbs

Contrast	**Result**	**Addition**	**Emphasis**
however	as a result	besides	indeed
instead	consequently	furthermore	in fact
nevertheless	hence	in addition	
on the other hand	therefore	moreover	

Conjunctive adverbs can be used in several ways. They can begin a sentence.

EXAMPLE *However,* I have always been interested in flags.

They can even be inserted in the middle of a sentence.

EXAMPLE I, *however*, have always been interested in flags.

When you use conjunctive adverbs to combine sentences, make sure that the two sentences contain ideas that are equally important. Each half of your combined sentence should be able to stand alone.

Original: I have always loved flags. They have become a passion lately.

Combined: I have always loved flags; *however*, they have become a passion lately.

NOTE: When you use conjunctive adverbs to join sentences, a semicolon comes before the conjunctive adverb and a comma comes after it.

Being able to use conjunctive adverbs effectively will help you to unify a piece of writing and make reading it an easy task.

DIRECTIONS Combine the sentences in each of the following numbered items.

- Use a conjunctive adverb to combine each numbered pair.
- When an italicized conjunctive adverb is not provided, choose the conjunctive adverb that makes the most sense.
- Make all changes on the worksheet. Use a caret (^) to indicate where words and punctuation should be inserted.

EXAMPLE During battles, soldiers would rally around their flag to protect it from the enemy; however, if the flag was captured, the soldiers would surrender.

(1) *Vexillology* means the study of flags. (Use *in fact.*) This word comes from the Latin *vexillum,* meaning a square flag or banner. **(2)** Many thousands of years ago, Egyptians flew the first flags. (Use *indeed.*) They probably tied streamers to poles and carried them into battle. **(3)** In battle, flags were important because generals could use them to locate their soldiers. (Use *furthermore.*) Flags identified enemy troops so that archers knew where to aim their arrows.

(4) Most national flags display one or more of seven basic colors. These colors have distinct meanings for the countries that use them. **(5)** The Danish flag has a white cross on a red field because a Danish king once saw a white cross in the red sky. The red and white of the Austrian flag derive from the bloodstained cloak and the belt of a crusader. **(6)** Five Central American countries were once united under a blue and white flag. Each of these independent countries now uses these colors in its national flag. **(7)** Blue, green, red, and white stand for Arab unity. These colors appear in the flags of both Jordan and Kuwait. **(8)** Often the stars on flags indicate unity. Stars may show how many individual states or provinces are united within a single country.

(9) No one knows who designed the flag of the United States. No one knows why the Continental Congress chose red, white, and blue for its colors. **(10)** The designers of the Great Seal of the United States, which also displays red, white, and blue, provided the meanings for these colors. We know that red means hardiness and courage, white means purity and innocence, and blue means vigilance, perseverance, and justice.

Using Adverb Clauses

Each year that you are in school, your studies will become more complex. Whether you know it or not, your thoughts and ideas are becoming more complex, too. Your writing should reflect your growing ability to master complicated relationships between ideas.

One easy way to express complex ideas is to use subordinating conjunctions to combine sentences.

Some Common Subordinating Conjunctions

after	as soon as	than	where
although	because	unless	wherever
as	if	until	whether
as if	so that	when	while

Subordinating conjunctions join sentences of unequal importance. When you use a subordinating conjunction, you create a subordinate clause. A **subordinate clause** (or ***dependent*** clause) does not express a complete thought and cannot stand alone.

Original: *Vacations are important.* Children often forget their studies in the summer.

Combined: *Although vacations are important,* children often forget their studies in the summer.

Original: Changes are not likely to come soon. *This issue is still hotly debated.*

Combined: Changes are not likely to come soon *because this issue is still hotly debated.*

NOTE: When a subordinate clause begins a sentence, the clause is followed by a comma. A subordinate clause at the end of a sentence does not need a comma.

DIRECTIONS Combine the following sets of sentences by using subordinating conjunctions.

EXAMPLE Consider both sides well, since this issue affects you.

Even though you may not believe it, you just might like a year-round school.

1. The traditional school calendar is based on the needs of an outdated farming economy. Many educators promote the idea of year-round school. (*because*)

2. The concept may not appeal to all students. Year-round school attendance could resolve the problem of overcrowded schools. (*even though*)

3. Some people would support year-round school. All schools had air conditioning. (*as long as*)

4. Few parents would want their children in hot classrooms. Summer is at its peak. (*when*)

5. Parents often support year-round schooling. They discover that long vacation breaks cause students to forget much of what they've learned. (*when*)

6. Year-round schooling is implemented. Students will have "mini-vacations" ranging from one to eight weeks. (*as soon as*)

7. In some areas, educators suggest year-round schooling. Additional programs and activities can be offered to students. (*so that*)

8. Several schedules have been proposed. One of the most popular plans under consideration would consist of forty-five days of school followed by fifteen days of vacation. (*Although*)

9. Researchers of year-round school scheduling agree that education will not improve. Improvement is everybody's primary concern. (*until*)

10. The 180-day school calender in the United States is shorter than that of any other industrialized nation. It may be that what is needed is not a different schedule, but a longer one. (*since*)

Choosing How to Combine

In these exercises, you are learning specific methods of combining sentences. However, in your own writing, your task will not be so easy. Any number of combinations may be possible.

Original: One mechanic changed the oil. Another mechanic checked the undercarriage.

- One mechanic changed the oil; another mechanic checked the undercarriage. (*combined using semicolon*)
- **As** one mechanic changed the oil, another checked the undercarriage. (*combined using a subordinating conjunction*)
- One mechanic changed the oil**, and** another checked the undercarriage. (*combined using a coordinating conjunction*)
- **Not only** did one mechanic change the oil, but another checked the undercarriage. (*combined using correlative conjunctions*)
- One mechanic changed the oil**; meanwhile,** another checked the undercarriage. (*combined using a conjunctive adverb*)
- The mechanics changed the oil **and** checked the undercarriage. (*combined using a compound verb*)

The method you choose will depend partly on the meaning and importance you want to give the ideas. Make a choice that gives style and variety to your writing.

DIRECTIONS For each of the following sets of sentences, create one complete sentence. Use any combining method you choose.

1. She felt as though she would never complete her research paper. Rene saw the number of library books she had piled up on the table.

2. She had just begun the research process. Her eyes were burning and her head was pounding.

3. Rene opened her English notebook. She noticed that the lecture notes were misplaced.

4. Rene read that research writing is a process. The steps are clearly defined.

5. Rene's deadline was approaching quickly. Her paper was in need of major revision.

6. Rene's eyes were glued to the computer screen. Her hands were typing rapidly.

NAME CLASS DATE

LESSON 15

Using Adjective Clauses

Adjective clauses can save you the trouble of writing a whole sentence to explain another sentence.

Original: Lise enjoys hearing the sounds of nature. *She lives on a farm.*

Combined: Lise, *who lives on a farm,* enjoys hearing the sounds of nature.

An **adjective clause** is a subordinate clause that modifies a noun or a pronoun. Adjective clauses usually begin with one of the following words.

that *where* *who* *whose* *when* *which* *whom*

In the example above, notice that one of these introductory words is positioned near the word or words that the adjective clause modifies.

NOTE: Clauses that can be omitted from a sentence without changing the meaning are called **nonessential** and set off with commas. Clauses that are **essential** to a sentence's meaning are not set off by commas.

Essential: The newspaper that I read every day is the *Chronicle.*

Nonessential: The *Chronicle,* which I read every day, is adding a sports section.

DIRECTIONS Combine the following sets of sentences by using adjective clauses. Add commas when necessary.

1. Jemma listens to music through a set of headphones when she is at work. She loves the blues. (*who*)

2. Antonio watches the games on TV with his pets. His two greyhounds seem to enjoy college football as much as he does. (*whose*)

3. When I was ready to leave the mall, I couldn't find the parking spot. I had parked my car in the spot. (*where*)

4. After looking for months, Raphael finally found a camera. He thought his father would like. (*that*)

5. In practice, the coach didn't notice our mistakes. We thought she was very thorough. (*whom*)

6. Martin's drive to work is twenty minutes each way. It takes him through the most congested streets in the city. (*which*)

Using Gerund Phrases

Without gerunds, we wouldn't have jogging, swimming, and collecting. Colleges wouldn't teach accounting. Speeding wouldn't be a problem on our highways, and nothing at all would be boring. Well, perhaps those things would exist, but we would have to call them something else because the names of each of these things are gerunds.

A **gerund** is a verb form ending in *-ing* that is used as a noun. A **gerund phrase** consists of a gerund and any modifiers and complements it may have. The entire gerund phrase acts as a noun. In other words, a gerund or a gerund phrase can do anything that a noun can do.

Subject: *Flying a plane* requires many hours of practice.
Indirect Object: Why don't you give *flying model planes* a trial period?
Direct Object: She loves *flying kites*.
Object of a Preposition: Tell us about *flying the glider in Colorado*, Dad.

Because gerunds are a verb form, they can add action to your sentences. Try using a gerund phrase to combine two choppy sentences. It will make a more direct statement.

Original: *I baby-sit neighborhood children*. I earn money that way.
Combined: I earn money by *baby-sitting neighborhood children*.
Combined: *Baby-sitting neighborhood children* is the way I make money.

Original: *They exercise every day*. This practice is their top priority.
Combined: *Exercising every day* is their top priority.
Combined: Their top priority is *exercising every day*.

Original: *We learned twenty Japanese words*. It was interesting.
Combined: *Learning twenty Japanese words* was interesting.

Notice that when you use a gerund phrase to combine sentences, you need to delete some words and change others. Be sure to read over your revision carefully to be sure that it makes sense and is correctly punctuated.

DIRECTIONS Combine each of the following sets of sentences into one sentence, using gerund phrases.

EXAMPLE He learned how to back up a trailer. The lesson took a half hour.

Learning how to back up a trailer took a half hour.

1. We practiced for the concert. It required patience and dedication.

2. The members of the committee argued over the issue for hours. This is how they finally reached an agreement.

____

3. My father votes in every election. He enjoys it.

____

4. I like to take my dog to Byrd park. We take walks there.

____

5. My friend Sarah listens to music. This is how she relaxes.

____

6. Scott sometimes mows yards after school. He earns money that way.

____

7. The group plays football every weekend. This is their favorite activity.

____

8. Our music teacher teaches guitar in the evenings. She earns extra money that way.

____

9. We read a Spanish folktale. It was interesting.

____

10. April passed her driver's test. It was easier than she had thought.

____

11. Many people fly kites in the summer. They enjoy it.

____

12. The pilot became interested in planes at an early age. He watched movies about flying.

____

13. My parents run in marathons. They consider it to be a healthy pastime.

____

14. Dogs often ride in cars. It can be a thrill for them.

____

15. I look through my telescope on clear nights. It is my favorite activity.

____

Using Infinitive Phrases

Infinitives and infinitive phrases are amazing. An infinitive phrase is probably the most versatile structure (besides sentences) in the English language. An infinitive phrase can actually be used as either a noun, an adjective or an adverb. If you learn to create an infinitive phrase, you'll have a quick and easy way to combine sentences.

An **infinitive** phrase is a verb form, usually preceded by *to*, that can be used as a noun, an adjective, or an adverb.

Noun: *To exit* is easy.
Adjective: This winter, red is the color *to wear*.
Adverb: *To exit*, press the F10 key.

An **infinitive phrase** consists of an infinitive together with its modifiers and complements. Believe it or not, the entire infinitive phrase can be used as a noun, an adjective, or an adverb.

Noun: Weren't you told *to report to the dugout*?
Adjective: The children will need something *to do this summer*.
Adverb: It is not hard *to remember the rules for tennis*.

Because infinitive phrases are so versatile, they are among the most powerful ways of combining sentences. After all, infinitive phrases can be used to answer just about any question that a reader might have—who, what, where, when, how, or why. When you use an infinitive to combine sentences, you can answer these questions before they even arise.

DIRECTIONS Use at least one infinitive phrase to combine each of the following sets of sentences into a single sentence.

EXAMPLES You can fix the printer. Just add ink.

To fix the printer, just add ink.

As a child, I had one dream. I wanted a horse.

As a child, my dream was to have a horse.

Be honest. You must know yourself.

To be honest, you must know yourself.

1. You will be writing a persuasive essay. You will need a topic that emotionally involves you.

2. My assignment was as follows. I must examine a social issue. I must also take a position on the topic.

3. Employers should hire disabled people. Employers should be encouraged to do so.

4. Some of us grow up with a disability. This experience confronts us with great challenges.

5. In my paper, I described the everyday lives of the disabled and focused on our employment opportunities. I wanted to do these things in my paper.

6. It required many hours of research and interviews. I accomplished this purpose.

7. I told their stories. I dispelled certain misconceptions. I met several people who wanted me to do these things in my paper.

8. You work for yourself. You are supported by others. Would you prefer one of these things over the other?

Using Noun Clauses

English is an amazing language: A whole group of words can function as a single part of speech. For example, a doctor's first, middle, and last name—as well as *Miss, Mrs.* or *Mr.* in front of the name and MD after the name—counts as a single noun.

You already know that a **noun** is a word used to name a person, place, thing or idea. A **noun clause** is a subordinate clause used as a noun. Noun clauses can appear anywhere that a noun can.

Subject: *What I learned* could fill a book.
Predicate Nominative: Basic documentation was *what I learned.*
Indirect Object: This assignment will give *what I learned* a chance to sink in.
Direct Object: She asked me *what I learned.*
Object of a Preposition: I could fill a book with *what I learned.*

When you use a noun clause to combine sentences, you will usually need to introduce the clause with one of the following words:

who *whom* *which* *what* *when* *where* *why* *how* *that*

Original: Aisya told me something. Our class is meeting in the library.
Combined: Aisya told me *that* our class is meeting in the library.
Aisya told me *when* our class is meeting in the library.
Aisya told me *whom* our class is meeting in the library.
Aisya told me *why* our class is meeting in the library.
Aisya told me *where* our class is meeting in the library.

When you use a noun clause to combine sentences, you can pack a lot of specific information in just one sentence, add variety to your sentence structures, and make your sentences more interesting.

DIRECTIONS On a separate sheet of paper, combine each set of items.

- For the first five items, use the italicized words to create noun clauses.
- For the last seven items, choose one of the introductory words above to create noun clauses.
- Insert each noun clause into an appropriate blank.

1. Ms. Herrera told us __________ and __________.
- Sources should be documented. (*why*)
- Documentation should be incorporated into our reports. (*how*)

2. She said ______________________.

- The documentation should be referenced on the works cited page. (*that*)

3. ______________ and ______________ were two topics addressed in class.

- We should make a source card. (*how*)
- We could ask for help at the library. (*whom*)

4. ______________ had never occurred to me.

- Bibliographic information is so important. (*why*)

5. Ms. Herrera explained ______________ and ______________.

- We should paraphrase a source. (*when*)
- We should use a direct quotation. (*when*)

6. Would you please show me ______________.

- I can make a works cited page from my source cards.

7. ______________ will help us to be better prepared for college.

- We learned in class.

8. With Ms. Herrera's guidance, we finally discovered ______________.

- We can paraphrase to improve our writing.

9. Our classed learned ______________ and ______________.

- Research is not always difficult.
- It can actually be fun.

10. ______________ and ______________ amaze me.

- So many students dread research papers.
- The process is actually easy.

11. With proper research techniques, you can discover ______________.

- Information is necessary to make your paper complete.

12. If the paper seems incomplete, you will know ______________.

- It is weak and needs support.

NAME ____________ CLASS ____________ DATE ____________

LESSON 19

Combining and Varying Sentences II

Imagine if all the sentences you read in a book started and ended the same way. Whether you realize it or not, it is usually the sentence structure that keeps you turning those pages of your favorite book.

DIRECTIONS Combine each of the following sets of sentences in two different ways, varying the beginnings of sentences.

1. Lisa Ortiz insists upon school uniforms. She is a candidate for class president. The other candidate, Marina Canales, says that they should not be mandatory.

2. We wrote an editorial. We spent hours perfecting our technique. The editorial persuaded students to vote.

3. The protesters stood outside. The judge sat quietly at his desk. The foreperson read the verdict.

4. Colin believes that some school policies should be changed. He maintains that students should write to the school newspaper to air their opinions.

5. Noah delivered his speech to the student body. Erika's eyes were fixed on her paper. Carlton's face was filled with concern.

NAME CLASS DATE

Combining Sentences to Write a Paragraph

DIRECTIONS Read the following sentences. Then, write a paragraph by using the facts and combining the sentences. The paragraph should describe writing a research paper.

1. A research paper is a written report that draws information from several sources.
2. It requires many steps.
3. Selecting a suitable topic is the first step in the process.
4. A topic is a subject that is neither too general nor too specific.
5. The best research papers capture the reader's attention.
6. The best research papers provide new, interesting information.
7. The library is not the only source of information.
8. It is the place where many people conduct their research.
9. You can interview experts who specialize in various subjects.
10. You can quote directly, summarize, or paraphrase.
11. You can use these methods when you take notes.
12. You need to make sure that all your notes clearly show the source.
13. Before writing, you should create a rough outline.
14. An outline is a list of headings and subheadings.